EAT THE GRAPES
DON'T FIGHT THE BATTLES

A MEMOIR OF A
TEACHER'S EXPERIENCE IN TURKEY

CRAIG R. JOHNSON

BEAVER'S
POND
PRESS

As a work of nonfiction, some names have been changed for
reasons of privacy.

ISBN 10: 1-59298-314-6
ISBN 13: 978-1-59298-314-8

Library of Congress Catalog Number: 2009937265

Printed in the United States of America

First Printing: 2010

14 13 12 11 10   5 4 3 2 1

Cover and interior design by James Monroe Design, LLC.

BEAVER'S
POND
PRESS

Beaver's Pond Press, Inc.
7104 Ohms Lane, Suite 101
Edina, MN 55439–2129
(952) 829-8818
www.BeaversPondPress.com

To order, visit www.BeaversPondBooks.com
or call (800) 901-3480. Reseller discounts available.

To Jean and Jennifer,
who were literally there for every step of the journey
and for every page of the book.

CONTENTS

Tell me a story.

In this century, and moment, of mania,
Tell me a story.

Make it a story of great distances, and starlight.

The name of the story will be Time,
But you must not pronounce its name.

Tell me a story of deep delight.

—*Robert Penn Warren*

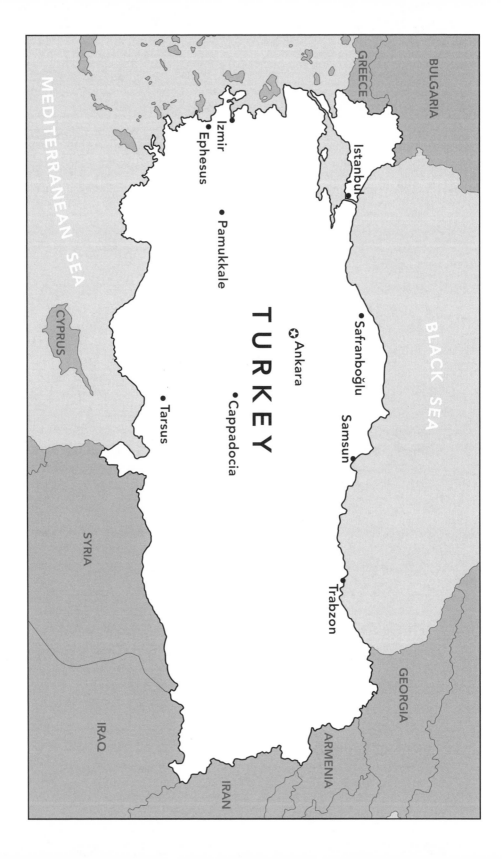

INTRODUCTION

My decision to resign from teaching and coaching was made with the desire to do something different with my life. I was not burned out after thirty-six years of coaching basketball and teaching physical education; I merely needed a change, which my current employment at a Minneapolis suburban high school could not provide. For me, to cease teaching would grant me the opportunity to explore, take risks, accept any failures, and, hopefully, enjoy the process. Although I generally enjoyed my profession, I was determined to prove to myself that life would have significance and purpose after retirement. I was not looking for a new career but simply a change. And yet, I had no specific plans.

To pursue this dream of change, I owe considerable thanks to my family, particularly, my wife Jean. She tends to see change from a different perspective than I, and change is not always comfortable for her. Her support, tolerance, respect, and love have not only allowed me to pursue my departure from the public school system, but also encouraged me to fulfill whatever was going on in my own little world. Any success I have in this phase of my life says more about her than it does about me.

My children—Craig, Kurt, and Jennifer—while not involved in specific decisions, were always encouraging and supportive, and often modeled many of the aspects of life that I was striving to accomplish. Learning from your kids—what a concept! At this time, our oldest son, Craig, was a new employee at a bond company in Minneapolis. He displayed a risk-taking nature when he volunteered to move to Chicago to work at a newly opened branch office. His advice to me was "Go for it!" Travel opportunities and the desire to help others led our second son, Kurt, to the Peace Corps. He was stationed in Nepal for two years. Jennifer, fifteen years old and about to enter two very important years of her high school life, shared her brothers' quest for opportunity and adventure. Suddenly, we were a family that was all about change.

Thoughts on Writing a Memoir

I doubt that anyone lives life in anticipation of writing a memoir. It may appear to some to be a bit presumptuous or egocentric. Yet, my view is that everyone should write his or her personal history. We all have a story to tell, so why not share it with others? I must admit that I did have a selfish motive as I began to talk about life and the experiences that change can offer. I hoped that in the writing of this memoir I would be creating more opportunities for myself; as a lifelong and still practicing procrastinator, writing things down encourages me to do more with my life.

How the Book was Written

Though I kept a journal from our first day in Turkey, a plan to initiate a book never entered my mind. My decision to record daily events was mostly to help me remember all that was happening. The notes were not for posterity. A simple recording, you could say. Gradually, I shifted my approach to writing about the emotions of the day. A typical day's pattern for my emotional state could easily range from euphoria to despair—all this on the way to school. The stimulation of this cultural onslaught was stressful at times. The writing seemed to relieve the stress somewhat, so I wrote more . . . day after day, page after page, the good and the bad. It was during our second year that I began to think that the family might enjoy reading these writings someday.

After returning to the United States, I was fired up. I jumped into volunteering—teaching both English-as-a-second-language and GED courses for single mothers in a welfare-to-work program. I also enrolled at the University of Minnesota for a political science class (confirming that I was conservative) and a linguistics class (where I hyperventilated during an open book test). Some say taking classes was all a guise to allow me to purchase student tickets for U of M basketball games. There is some truth to that statement. Eventually, I registered for a "Writing Your Memoirs" class with an assortment of middle-aged folks and a teacher-author-mentor who provided the relaxed atmosphere that I needed. That is until one day we were instructed to read aloud several pages of our developing manuscript. That was a tense moment, but receiving some positive feedback, the idea of a book was formulated.

The teacher recommended that I change the format from a daily journal to one of relating stories that flowed with developing narrative. This suggestion raised some fears, which led to apprehension. The book idea lay idle for about four years.

I woke up one morning and read an article about a book publishing company in the morning paper. The fact that they specialized in mentoring neophyte authors caught my interest. A phone call to Milt Adams, the founder, led to some discussion and a meeting with more feedback—and a book was born.

I have made a genuine attempt to write this book for the right reason, which is to share with you, the reader, the experience of our two years in Turkey. I wanted to give an accurate and honest account, and, hopefully, bring you along with us. I wanted you to share vicariously in a fascinating, at times frustrating, and always interesting adventure—years that turned out to be the two richest years of my life.

The Story

This book is a tour through the culture of Turkey and beyond. It's a look into life from the view of a foreign visitor and the whimsy that can be found only among the young and, in this instance, at a school. Our family attempted from the beginning to learn from our experience and make it positive. As Henry David Thoreau said, "To affect the quality of the day, that is the highest of the arts." To what degree we were able to do this is up for analysis. That was the goal, however. None of our frustrations or problems was ever allowed to become a permanent concern or issue. We were always able to sort things out or solve them with help. The stimulation and excitement of living in Turkey, in fact, completely overwhelmed any problems or predicaments, making this endeavor a once-in-a-lifetime opportunity.

Based on this experience, I have gained a greater appreciation for the world and its people. This is nothing new, I am certain. But prior to Turkey, I lived with a domestic mindset. Even as an avid newspaper reader, I merely glanced at the international news section. Now my interest has been heightened; I want to know about the world, and I want to understand my responsibility in it.

PRE-GAME

Life can be like a ball game. There is a beginning, an end, and lots of action in between. You have a game plan and implement it as best you can. Or things can really go bad and you need to stop, step back, and call a timeout. You may even need to change your strategy. Sometimes there's a jump ball, which means the game stops, forcing you to put the ball into play again.

That was where I was; I needed to start over with a new plan.

The only plan I had for a job change was to try just about anything, accept the possibility that I might fail and, hopefully, find opportunities that would be meaningful. This was my thinking as I headed into a new phase of life: "Make it happen . . . make it a good day."

IT'S NOT OVER YET—ONE MAN'S VIEW

I had a decision to make. I was fifty-seven years young, with one son, Craig, graduated and on his own; a second son, Kurt, a senior at the University of Virginia; and, Jennifer, starting her ninth year in school.

In October of 1994, Jean, Jennifer, and I went to Galena, Illinois, for a long weekend. One evening while walking on the bank of the local river, I asked Jean's opinion of my taking an early retirement from coaching basketball and teaching high school.

"What will you do?" she asked.

"What about money?"

"Why? Are you angry with someone at school?"

My responses in order were: "I'm not sure." "We don't have much." "I just want a change."

The pace of our walk was easy, but my heart was racing as I shared my feelings regarding early retirement. I was the fast-talking salesman, excited about my product and trying to close the deal. I was the coach motivating his underdog team for the big game. I was the military leader explaining the course of action that could determine the fate of the upcoming battle. Well, you get the idea. I was really pumped about the prospect of job change, and it was very important to convey that message.

I think she said "Yes."

Just knowing that my family supported my desire to change lifted the yoke that confined me to my daily school routine. My pending resignation excited me. I was beginning to feel free . . . and it felt good.

Let me clarify that my chosen profession for thirty-some years had been satisfying and rewarding. While I had never really looked at teaching high school and coaching basketball as a job, I enjoyed it more in my early years when I moved around every two or three years to a new school, new people, and a new town. Though I had taken two sabbaticals for renewal at the college level, I determined that high school was best for me. Yet, now, I felt stuck. I needed another sabbatical—a long one.

A career change is not an easy decision, even when you are motivated. Sam Keen wrote in an essay that leaving home for the first time is a big deal. He calls it the biggest and most difficult *no* in our lives. Saying *no* to security, comfort, and convenience is not easy. As most of us have learned, however, it is very necessary and important to our development and sense of responsibility to leave home. I suggest that taking early retirement is just as big and difficult a *no* in our lives. When we retire, we are saying *no* to the comfort and security of a long-time career. We are saying good-bye to the ease of going to the workplace where we are in control. We may even grieve the loss of financial security and the prestige of a long-time position. This can be true, regardless of the work situation. I am just suggesting that even when all the pieces are in place to make a change, it isn't easy.

I Did It—I Resigned

Jean didn't fully understand my feelings about a job change, but from the day we talked in Galena until I officially retired, I was obsessed. Similar to the feelings I have when I want a new car or some other masculine toy, I awoke each morning feeling refreshed having dreamed of life as a retiree. While standing in the front of any given class, I would smile to myself, thinking, "You students don't know this, but I am going to stop teaching, and very soon!" Third-person thoughts began to pop into my head such as, "Here comes Craig Johnson. He's going to retire soon. He's going to quit teaching and then. . . . " Well, as I mentioned earlier, I didn't have any definitive plans.

Admittedly, these thoughts were clouding my objectivity. I wasn't exactly tormented, but resignation notions became more and more intrusive. Finally, without further discussion with Jean, and just before Christmas, I walked unannounced into the principal's office and told him I wanted to retire after Christmas.

At his desk, pen in hand, he said, "That will be fine."

How could he be so unemotional on one of the biggest days of my life? I astutely sensed that this news wouldn't ruin his day. He didn't even say, "Why don't you wait until the end of the school year?"

My heart rate was soaring as I left his office. I was euphoric. I felt a sense of freedom that I hadn't experienced since I was a young boy in Benson, Minnesota, on the first day of summer vacation. No cares, no worries.

Reality quickly resurfaced when I walked into our home and greeted Jean with, "I resigned today. I am retiring after Christmas."

At the sink, rinsing vegetables for dinner, she whirled around. "You're what?"

Questions flooded my addled brain. Hadn't we talked about this? Wasn't this agreed upon? Isn't she happy for me?

After a short conversation, Jean's initial shock wore off. The great communicator was at work again.

On January 4, 1995, I spent my first day of retirement in my pajamas. The weather was cold, I couldn't decide what to wear, and I had nowhere to go (at least until basketball practice at 4:30, as I would continue coaching). The day was one of the longest and loneliest of my life.

Life after Teaching, Or What am I Going to Do Now?

Two weeks later, still in my pajamas on a cold morning, an ad in the newspaper caught my eye: "Wanted: A Teacher to Teach Car Sales Staff." Friendly Chevrolet in Fridley was interviewing teachers to instruct sales staff on the latest car features. I interviewed, they observed me teaching a mock lesson, and I got the job. I knew nothing about car features, but I did know how to teach. With a number of gimmicks, I was able to motivate the always-competitive sales staff with gift certificates of dinners, golf outings, and assorted discounts to the students with the best scores. A few of them even made the connection that learning about car features increased their sales and commission. After each lesson and subsequent test, I would correct the papers and, with scores in hand, enter the sales floor. Typically, the salespeople, with an innocent eagerness that had long been neglected, rushed to me for their scores. It should be noted here that they did not necessarily like me or the time spent in class, but both were tolerated.

I might not have known much about cars, but the program was successful in spite of my ignorance. Since that time, for ten straight years (without me), Friendly Chevrolet has been ranked the number one Chevy volume dealer in the metropolitan Twin Cities.

That summer, I also worked at a local country club and at first I was certain that I had found the perfect job. I was a ranger and a pro shop clerk. There were conflicts, however; when I was driving the course as a ranger to encourage faster play, I wished that I were playing. When I was in the pro shop, I yearned to be outside. Overall, I must give myself a low grade. During one ill-fated episode, I spent close to an hour trying to fit a seventy-three-year-old man into a size seven woman's golf shoe. A "D" would also be an appropriate grade when I think of my inability to master the pro shop computer register. All sales were charges, and there was a ten-step process to complete a computer transaction. I could only remember five steps. I would often find myself discouraging club members from making a purchase due to my inadequacies in recording a sale. In other words, I was bad for business. I was personable but incompetent.

While my business career was floundering, I was writing letters to all the people I knew around the world—which in total was three. In response to one of those letters, I traveled to Australia in pursuit of a basketball coaching job. The position would entail coaching a club team in Cairns and developing a youth program. That job may have been the answer to my dreams, but failure to acquire a work visa dimmed the prospect. We were all disappointed.

A Job Offer

Shortly before Christmas 1995, we heard about an international teaching job fair at the University of Northern Iowa. We were told that it was quite late to apply and that we might not receive all the benefits of early registration. Early registrants had the advantage of having their credentials available for perusal by school personnel. Jean and I saw evidence of this when we arrived at the job fair in February and were not scheduled for any preliminary interviews, while early applicants had ten or more. As a result, we revised our plan, deciding that we would merely get a feel for the situation. We would look around, ask questions, and come back in an earnest job search the following year.

The job fair was an event that moved me in ways that few have in my life. The Final Four ranks high, but the impact of this event was completely unexpected. (A job fair is not a highly charged sports event or spiritual gathering.)

The huge room was filled to capacity with over nine hundred international job seekers. Their enthusiasm fully embraced us when the convener dismissed us from the general assembly to the converted ballroom. The room was lined with tables representing various schools, all manned by superintendents and representatives from schools around the world. We were overwhelmed with the room's energy and awestruck by the mass of people seeking their destiny. I had no idea that there was such a market for international teaching. Those present appeared to be experienced overseas teachers, although I did run into an old college classmate who was also new to the scene. (And wouldn't you know that he and I wound up vying for the same job.)

The schools were presented in alphabetical order, so the first place we stopped was The American Collegiate Institute located in Izmir, Turkey. A small handwritten sign, indicating the need for a computer teacher and a physical education teacher and department head, caught my attention.

"Hey Jean," I said, "That's us!" Jean was a computer consultant who had formerly been a business teacher.

The school's director, Dr. Stenberg, a gray-haired man with glasses, greeted us. "Sign up here if you would like to interview later this afternoon. I have an opening at three." We spoke briefly, signed up, and moved on. This was easy, I thought.

We wove through crowds of people, moving from booth to booth. Our hopes of finding positions suitable for both of us were fading when Dr. Stenberg reappeared, remarking that after looking over our credentials, he was surprised that he had missed us during his initial search of prospects. He appeared interested.

In smaller rooms throughout the building, school personnel were conducting narratives and slide shows depicting the physical features of their schools, curriculums, and cities. In our excitement, we randomly jumped from room to room, catching a glimpse of the exotic places we had only read about in magazines. We were captivated by the visual accounts on Bangkok, Hong Kong, and Germany; it was difficult to comprehend that places like that could be an option for us.

Finally 3:00 p.m. rolled around, and we sat down with Dr. Stenberg from Turkey. The reserved man with the professorial look didn't ask us many questions, but instead spent most of the time selling his school's virtues. That struck me as strange. Suddenly the interview was over, and I felt I had not been given the chance to expound on my philosophy of education or theories of learning. I had not participated in a job interview in twenty-five years; I was disappointed and believed that I had blown our big chance. Oh well, there was always next year.

That evening at dinner, Jean and I excitedly discussed the prospects of living and teaching overseas. We found it easy to fantasize even when we hadn't been presented with an offer.

Well, okay, I was excited; Jean contained herself. But we did have a mutual interest in any adventures that lay ahead. At this point, I strongly believed that my life would be unfulfilled without the experience of living abroad.

The message machine was blinking when we returned to our room. It was a message from Dr. Stenberg asking us to please call him as soon as we returned, as he would be working late. "Let's wait until morning," said Jean. I agreed, probably out of fear and apprehension.

The phone rang at 7:15 a.m., awakening me from a night of intermittent sleep. Dr. Stenberg got right to the point: "I would like to offer you and Jean jobs in Turkey."

I hoped that he didn't hear me gasp. He continued. "Are you both interested?" I was ready to jump on the plane, but Jean's expression and tense body language implied something totally different.

After a heavy pause, I calmly responded, "We are very interested but need to talk with our daughter." Jean was now as white as the bed sheet wrapped around her.

He said that he understood and asked us to meet him for breakfast, where he explained some of the intricacies of the contracts. Up to this point, it was my understanding that all foreign teaching took place at international schools for students whose parents worked abroad. Our teaching contracts, however, would place us in a private school for Turkish students only—students who were immersed in English upon entering as sixth graders. Jean would be teaching computer classes and keyboarding to all grade levels. She would be part of a teaching staff of three and would be the only foreigner. My job would be the Physical Education Department head, Prep (sixth grade) teacher, athletic director, and basketball coach. Being the replacement for a man who left in the middle of the previous year could be challenging. His decision to leave had created some turmoil, which left the department with a dysfunctional label.

As we drove back home to Minneapolis, we made small talk about Turkey. Our emotions loomed large; fear and excitement took up much of the room in the car.

Here we were, driving along talking about moving to Turkey. Turkey, of all places! Who lives there? Where is it exactly? Is it safe? Our conversation went something like this:

Craig: "What an experience this will be!"

Jean: "My consulting business will be finished."

Craig: "We'll rent the house."

Jean: "I'm not sure about having someone live in my house."

Craig: "We'll see the world."

Jean: "I'm afraid to fly."

I could barely contain myself; Jean had no trouble at all.

Family concerns came to mind. Son Craig had just moved to Chicago; Kurt was in the Peace Corps in Nepal; Jen was a sophomore in high school; my mother was eighty-three years old. What affect would this have on each of them?

Jennifer was at the kitchen table when we walked into the house. I was on an emotional high, and Jean was just plain emotional. She could say little, however, to deter my enthusiasm. "We have a job offer," I blurted out. "Guess where."

Jennifer went through a series of countries: Scotland? England? France? Germany? When I finally said, "Turkey," she exclaimed, "Turkey? Where is Turkey?"

And that began a series of family meetings and discussions that went on for days. I didn't care where we went (so much for discernment), but we did have to find answers for several questions regarding safety, school standards, accreditation, and what the city of Izmir had to offer.

How does one make a decision to move to a foreign country in just a few days? Do you use your logic and reasoning powers honed over a lifetime? Unfortunately our pros-and-cons list just didn't cut it. Do you ask all your friends who have lived in Turkey? Yeah, right. Basically, you make your decision based on your instincts and your emotions. Our decision to go to Turkey turned out to be just that, an emotional decision. Going felt like the right thing to do. In my mind, not going would have been a fateful mistake. Jennifer agreed and Jean went along, though with reservations. I must admit that the decision felt comfortable for me after many years of being logical and judicious in my thinking. Job change—life change—was beginning to make sense and feel good.

Now that our decision was made, it was time to put the hoopla behind us and get serious. During the next few weeks we filled out many forms for the Turkish Ministry and for the school where we would teach. My emotions slid back and forth between euphoria and fear. On March 25, despite the delays and the complexity of Turkish bureaucracy, the final approval arrived in our mailbox.

How About Some Turkey?

I appreciated the willingness and sacrifices that Jean and Jen were making to satisfy my enthusiasm. Jean had worked hard creating a freelance computer training business focused on presenting new programs and techniques to businesses and teachers. It was stressful at times, but rewarding. Jennifer would have to say goodbye to the last two years of high school and to lifelong friends. She had started school in Wayzata as a kindergartner; her best friends were three girls living within one block. This move was a lot to ask from both of them. As for me, I was giving up the attractive but empty life of a retiree, who had no plan or clue as to what he was doing with this important part of his life.

To complicate our decision, days before we were to sign our Turkish contract, we received a call from Australia with the news that the work visa we had applied for had at last been approved. Suddenly we had a choice: Australia or Turkey? We voted. The vote was three to zero that we continue on the path to Turkey, which would provide an enhanced cultural experience and greater job stability for both of us. Jean would have had to find work in Australia, and I didn't want to coach full time.

I asked myself these questions almost daily: Was it fair of me to take my family thousands of miles away to live and work in a foreign land? Was it a good idea to leave my mother behind (although she had been independent for the past forty years)? I was asking the right guy because my answer always came back with a resounding "Yes!" I believed that this experience would be extraordinary, exciting, and maybe a little crazy. More importantly, it would be full of the unknown. The three of us would be together. Regardless of any circumstances or problems, we would view this two-year experience as positive. We would make it a good two years.

"You're going where?" people asked. When I answered "Turkey," the next one-word question was always "Why?" with a grim, sometimes sad, tight-lipped shake of the head. When one makes a decision to leave home as we did, one should not bank on support from family and friends. I did not need their affirmation, and that was a good thing, but Jean needed reassurance and positive support, which rarely occurred. At times, this was difficult for her.

We talked daily about our move and came to understand that this opportunity was a chance for serious growth. My feeling was that if you believe in yourself, want to do something that is right for you, and are doing it for the right reason, you don't need the approval of others. It also became apparent that we needed each other more than before, and that this need would undoubtedly increase.

Preliminary work was time consuming but easy. Passports, medical reports, and credentials were completed and sent by June.

The heavy stuff—renting our home, selling our cars, storing our furniture, and updating our will—was overwhelming.

I decided to advertise and manage the rental of our house myself, as opposed to hiring a home rental agency. While a few want ads brought in some calls, a hand-painted sign in the yard proved most successful. We ultimately rented our home to a couple moving to Minneapolis from Memphis. He was moving his dental laboratory business to the Twin Cities, and they liked our area. She was going to write a book. An old friend, Lynn, agreed to manage the property and make homeowner decisions that could arise during the two years we were away. That gave us some comfort as we relinquished possession.

Jean was away at work during the day, so Jennifer and I held our first garage sale solo. Our going-to-Turkey sale proved to be an effective way to clean out the closets, basement, and garage after fifteen years of accumulation, American style.

Then the work truly began. Moving is hard work, but moving and not bringing our possessions with us was tricky. We packed what we thought would be suitable clothing, potential teaching materials, and miscellaneous must-have items. We stored as much of our furniture as we thought we could safely stuff into our largest bedroom over the garage. At times the vision of our treasured belongings breaking through the bedroom floor and ending up in a heap down below entered my mind.

The preparation heightened in intensity after our airplane tickets arrived. It was too late to back out now. July was a whirlwind of activity as we made time for good-byes with family and friends. We encouraged visits to Turkey, but no one seemed too excited about the prospect. If only they had studied Turkish in college.

GOOD-BYE AMERICA,
MERHABA TÜRKIYE!

The big black SUV backed into the driveway. Stress and anxiety were high as we bid our family and friends good-bye. I closed the door on our neighbor's Suburban and settled back into my seat, feeling a strange combination of freedom and relief. How could that be? I was leaving my homeland for a foreign culture that was rife with unknowns. I had anticipated more anxiety than relief. Maybe there was comfort in denial.

With one of our fourteen pieces of luggage in my lap and another gently nudging the back of my head, I felt a calmness that can only come from being relieved of the burden of responsibility that accompanies a typical American husband, father, and wage earner. As the truck door closed, I felt reassured of my decision.

My wife and daughter sat in the backseat amidst mounds of luggage. Jean was exhausted from the last few days of cleaning, packing, and working through the night. Tears had welled up, and she looked more than apprehensive. Was it her fear of flying or the stress of turning over her home to strangers in exchange for an uncertain situation in Turkey? I wasn't sure and I didn't ask.

Jennifer looked a bit dazed as she stared straight ahead. She showed no emotion and had a vacant look in her eyes. As a sixteen-year-old girl whose interests and abilities ranged from music to literature to athletics, moving to Turkey may have been more than a bit daunting. She had fully agreed to the adventure, but the question of fairness at this stage of her life continued to haunt me.

All of a sudden my head was buzzing. Guilt will do that. The calmness I had initially felt was a result of successfully dealing with the superficial things such as renting our house, selling our cars, storing our furniture, and saying good-bye to the routine of life. My guilt escalated as the important matters of safety, relationships, and emotional well-being clouded my thoughts.

Consequently, the ride to the airport became quieter. I found myself repeating the mantra, "We will make this a good experience."

What I should have been thinking about was our arrival at the airport where we would be faced with the task of maneuvering fourteen bags to the international ticket counter. These were not normal bags but rather over-sized and over-stuffed duffel bags containing our belongings for the next two years.

We gave Peggy, our neighbor-turned-chauffeur, a couple of hurried reminders regarding last-minute details at home. She offered a hug, and we returned heartfelt thanks as we watched her pull away from the curb. We were on our own, and there was no turning back.

Recounting our fourteen bags for the fifth time, I relived the image of Jennifer's friends crying in the driveway as we pulled away. A baggage attendant interrupted my counting, asking if he could help. With relief, I helped him stack the bulk of our bags on his cart. We carried the remainder as we wove and stumbled our way through the crowd. We felt fortunate and a little obvious as our attendant marched us right to the front of the line. Our bags were quickly processed, and we were given our boarding passes. Reaching into my pocket, I found a handful of loose bills that I gratefully gave to the porter. I wanted to hug him but didn't. A casual look back at the long line of people made me feel like a seasoned traveler, or a mountain climber peering down from the summit at the stragglers yet to reach their goal. I was beginning to feel calm and relaxed about this travel thing.

The early morning layover in Frankfurt, Germany, revealed a nearly vacant waiting area. We were all feeling the effects of having flown through the night. I observed a couple with a teenage daughter sitting nearby who were about our age. I was either too weary or too reserved to ask them if they were going to Turkey. But then again, what were the odds?

Bring on the Turks!

Hours later, we were back in the air approaching Izmir, Turkey. As the wings of the plane dipped, I saw rugged, barren land with few trees or flourishing crops, the opposite of what we had left in green, lush, woodsy Minnesota. Where were the palm trees, the picturesque harbor, and the boats that had been featured in the brochures? My views from the air were substantiated as we touched the ground. The reading material had described the third largest city in Turkey as a modern metropolis overlooking the Aegean Sea. What I saw appeared desert-like and desolate. My heart sank as I repeated what was now becoming a worn-out expression: "We'll make the best of this experience and grow in the process."

Hesitantly, I took my first step off the plane and into the heat of the August midday sun. The 150-foot walk from the plane to the airport terminal produced a mixture of sweat and nausea. We were maneuvered through customs to a small baggage claim area that was as steamy as the tarmac outside. Everyone looked very foreign . . . until an upright and pleasant-looking young man approached us.

Andrew, the school's foreign-faculty representative, welcomed us warmly. We were drawn to him as though he were an old friend. I wanted to ask him the whereabouts of the flora and fauna he had so artfully described to us in one of the many letters previously written, but decided against it.

I began pulling bag after bag from the faltering carousel. My fear of lost bags was not realized, and I beamed with a perverse sense of pride as the stack of duffel bags grew. Jennifer quickly reminded me of just how embarrassing it was to have so many bags!

Across the terminal, two other prospective teachers were also collecting their bags. But wait, they didn't have bags, they had boxes. Did they have boxes!

We introduced ourselves to Jeff, Jackie, and Tessa from Canada and to Wayne, Andee, and Colby from Missouri. We eyed each other's accumulation of stuff, and Jennifer seemed pleased that their piles were higher and assuredly more cumbersome. At least one person could lift any one of ours.

We moved easily through security and customs. Our new friends, however, had brought several electronic items that required inspection. The rule in Turkey is that when you bring something electronic into the country, you must take it with you when you leave; hence, the need for inspection. The inspection was thorough, precise, and not at all careful. These boxes would never be used again for their original purpose; they were sliced open and maimed as item after item was removed. Jean's decision to carry on her new laptop precluded her from the inspection process.

The tension grew as the interested parties observed the semi-destructive inspection. Much shouting and language interpretation and misinterpretation took place. Thankfully, one of the prerequisites for the foreign faculty representative was the ability to speak Turkish. Andrew stepped in when the language became as hot as the temperature, and his hard-core negotiating stopped the inspectors from going through every box. An hour or so later, the items were replaced and the boxes retaped.

Andrew made a few more introductions, including Dr. Stenberg, the director who hired us. How nice, I thought, that he cares enough to come out on this hot and humid day.

"We are so happy to have the Johnsons here with us," was

the comment I heard first.

Director Stenberg invited us all to a welcome-to-Turkey party that evening. "That will be a good opportunity for everyone to meet Dr. Thompson, the new director." New director? No one had informed us! I was shocked and very disappointed as I had come to work for the man who had hired us, not a stranger who didn't know our background.

Jean quietly, but with an anxious look, said, "Does it bother you that the man who hired us is leaving and they wait until now to tell us?"

I couldn't muster a valid response, except, "That must be the way they do things here." These words would prove to be prophetic.

The introductions continued as we approached three smiling, dark-haired, dressed-for-labor men, all from the school. Their mission was to move all of our belongings. The swarthiest of the three extended a welcoming hand, switching the cluster of grapes he was eating to his other hand. He smiled warmly, the ends of his prominent mustache curling upward. "*Merhaba, hoşgeldiniz*," he said. In English, I responded, "Thank you, it's my pleasure." I was hoping he had greeted me with hello.

That was the beginning of what would become many conversations with Turks where both parties could only assume what had actually been said.

A pickup truck, with sideboards, pulled up to the airport entrance. The large boxes—you remember them—were loaded first. They were further abused as box after box was wedged into place. The truck was now piled with boxes well above the sideboards.

Where was the second truck parked? There wasn't one in sight. "What about my bags?" I sounded whiny, but I was concerned. "There is no room."

My new worker friend, though still swarthy, was now grape-less. He confidently replied in broken English, "No problem, no problem." This was a phrase that would be repeated often over the next two years.

He reached into the cab of the truck as he spoke. Back he came with a series of ropes and that bright smile. The other workers began tossing our overstuffed duffel bags on top of the boxes. Another worker jumped atop to stabilize (a euphemism) the situation. Round and round the rope went. Knotted here and there, bags were stomped and squeezed when deemed necessary. Finally all fourteen bags were mostly on the truck; a few drooped over the sides. The shape of the truck cargo resembled a precarious mushroom, one surely doomed. I was worried and my worry was justified.

In the United States, it was both illegal and illogical to do what we were setting out to do. In Turkey, this overloaded conveyance appeared to be no problem. We piled into a van to trail the truck on our trek to our new home. I was perspiring from the heat and from being forced to watch what, to me, seemed inevitable. We drove off in the crowded van with the "mushroom" truck just ahead. The advantage of trailing behind was to rescue each piece of luggage when it fell off the truck. But not to worry . . . we lost sight of the truck five minutes into the drive.

The traffic on the busy streets of Izmir was intense and chaotic. I welcomed the diversion of studying the city's buildings. Lining the road were numerous four-story buildings with the top two floors unfinished. The blocks appeared ready to be set in place, but on second glance, it was obvious that they had been that way for years. Unfinished architecture would become a common sight for us throughout Turkey. The shops appeared to be small and shabby. The buildings looked cold, block-like, and without character. We knew that Izmir sat on a bay, but what we had seen was more reminiscent of a desert. Though we had been told that Izmir was the most modern and beautiful city in Turkey, our first impression did not match that description.

Traffic was hampered with severe congestion and a casual disregard for proper lane usage, which encouraged drivers to honk their horn with routine vigor. It appeared that straddling lanes was accepted and encouraged. To an uptight visitor peeking out of the dirty window of the van, to be in the middle of such a throng was crazy, scary, and a bit exciting. Once again, this was not what I expected.

The streets, crowded with people, created a lively ambiance. Men linked arm in arm walked the dusty, uneven streets and sidewalks in animated discussion. Many were gesturing in a manner that appeared positive. Seemingly heedless of the mounting temperatures, they were dressed in semi-formal fashion, including hats and jackets. We later learned that many were coming or going to their favorite tea house to play a game of dominoes or cards.

The women dressed in varying styles. In the outlying communities near the airport, many wore veils and were fully covered. Small shops sold their wares, and a perpetual display of colorful scarves waved to us as we passed by, enticing us to stop. As we traveled closer to the downtown area, the dress became more European.

Periodically, when I turned my eyes away from the activity that surrounded us, I scanned the road for fallen duffel bags or for an overstuffed truck stopped to secure its cargo. Nothing yet, and my thoughts turned to the practical:

- Do they have insurance in Turkey?

- Do they sell extra tall men's clothing?

- Why didn't we pack our belongings in sturdy boxes?

- How can we make this adventure a positive experience?

- Why is Jean looking at me with that what-have-you-gotten-us-into look?

- Am I going to see that look often in the next two years?

Abruptly, we turned from the horde of traffic into a gated compound where we found an unlikely oasis of green, coupled with wisteria, roses, bougainvillea, and other colorful flowers. A gratifying sight indeed, but it failed to measure up to what followed. Once inside the campus we recognized the long lost, but not forgotten, truck. Its mushroom-shape was still intact and the three smiling workmen proudly stood watch. They gave us the universal thumbs-up sign that seemed to say, "No problem, no problem."

Our Home Away From Home

One family at a time was escorted to their apartment. I thought we would go first because our luggage was on top. No, not the plan; we were last. I had formerly pictured a private upstairs apartment on a quaint tree-lined street. What makes a person do that to himself? Why create such expectations?

What we found was a flat in a drab, concrete apartment building on a very dusty street with the nearest tree blocks away. The apartment was about sixty feet long and twelve-thirteen feet wide. The bowling alley shape did not lend itself to coziness, and it was not particularly clean.

The third-floor apartment had a good-sized living and dining room area. The window at the front of the apartment opened to a small balcony, which looked down on the street. The combination living-and-dining room was graced with an eight-foot-long table topped off with a plastic flowery tablecloth, which was reminiscent of my childhood. We found the high-backed chairs surrounding the table fragile when moved. In fact, we would later find the chair backs susceptible to collapsing when someone leaned back to relax. We were fortunate to have two sofas, but the mismatched plaid upholstery was unattractive, and the comfort level wasn't up to par. So, there was an irreconcilable fashion conflict going on between the sofas, the flower-laden tablecloth, and the Turkish carpets.

Along the longest hallway in Turkey was a small kitchen, a bathroom, a half bath, and a windowless room that would become Jennifer's. The end of the hallway diverged into two rooms. It was our choice as to which one would become the master bedroom and which would become the spare room. Our pick was negotiable as one had a closet and one had a small balcony. We chose the room with the balcony as we thought the slight breeze would make sleeping more comfortable. What we didn't know was that the balcony's open door would also enable us to more clearly hear the 5:00 a.m. Call to Prayer.

The workers from the school delivered all fourteen of our bags, and we were left tired, lonely, demoralized, and surely disappointed. We looked at each other; I had the good sense to say nothing.

Jean spoke quietly. "Craig, you take the bags back to the bedroom, and Jennifer and I will start to scrub."

As I dragged our bags down the long hallway, my confidence was shaken. I needed a pep talk. Could we make this a good experience?

We were scrubbing down the kitchen when we saw our first cockroach. Boy they're quick! We later learned that our friends from Canada had found an extremely large cockroach in their bedroom. Their family joined forces and slept together the first night.

We worked hard. We prepared our beds and scrubbed the floors and walls. We took the drawers out of their respective spaces and literally doused them with boiling hot water on the back balcony. It should be noted that our clothes and items were ultimately placed in clean and spotless drawers. It should also be noted that all the drawers became warped and never closed properly again. It should further be noted that this scrubbing was not my idea. But we all felt sure that when we were to return later that night, we could sleep well, as I always sleep better when the drawers are clean.

We set our watches to Turkish time and left the apartment just before six in the evening for the new teacher orientation. Quiet, tired, and reflective of the day's events, we walked down a steep, narrow, winding road to the alumni house.

The warm evening welcomed us to the courtyard of an old, restored Ottoman mansion named The Blake House. Rose bushes and various other flowers in full bloom surrounded the house. The beautiful setting was well maintained. I soon found myself hungrily eating and enjoying Turkish *meze* (appetizers). The new teachers, eight in all, seemed friendly, diverse, and excited about the prospect of teaching in Turkey. Everyone introduced himself or herself by sharing an anecdote. The wine and the general excitement of gathering with new friends from around the world eased the weariness and anxiety we'd been feeling. At the end of the evening, as the three of us walked back up the hill and home, we felt better. Traces of excitement were returning, and fears and disappointments were retreating.

Another Slice of Turkey

As we waited for the bus for an abbreviated tour of Izmir, we received an introduction to Turkish justice from a civilian point of view. A loud shriek followed by continued wailing erupted from outside the campus gate. The distress was coming from an older woman who had just had her purse snatched. We were making an attempt to comfort her when two young males rushed up to hear her story. They hurried off. Within minutes, the two young men came swaggering back carrying a purse and flanking a third person, the alleged thief.

They dragged him up to the woman. She grabbed her purse and pummeled the robber around the head with it. Wow! She was feisty and angry. Quickly the two men dragged him off to the police station before she could finish her assault.

We asked the foreign faculty advisor what would happen to the robber. "He probably will be beaten and placed in jail," he said.

This was an interesting first look at law and order, Turkish style.

The foreign faculty advisor was our guide for the day. Andrew herded us onto the bus for a short two-block drive to the long awaited view of the Aegean Sea. It was a welcoming sight and, yes, there were palm trees along the esplanade. Izmir's harbor formed a natural half-moon fortified with miles and miles of concrete wall and backed by mountains in the south and east. Crowded ferries dotted the water, indicating that it was a viable transportation mode. The streets were crowded with plentiful small shops and cafés on the first level giving rise to apartments up to five floors high. Izmir, formerly Smyrna, is an ancient-turned-modern city that has been rebuilt numerous times due to fires, earthquakes, and wars. It is also the leading port on the Aegean. Except for Coca-Cola signs, the advertising was in Turkish. There was nothing western about the look, feel, and smell of the city. We briefly visited the city center, Alsancak, where the financial district, government buildings, and entertainment were housed. Wide streets and modern buildings pointed out the newer construction of the third largest city in Turkey.

Andrew then casually informed us that we would be going to Istanbul that night for a week of orientation. The bad news was that we would be traveling by bus. The orientation would include new teachers from the sister schools in Istanbul and Tarsus. Our bus was to leave Izmir at midnight and arrive in Istanbul around 7:00 a.m.

The hot, dusty, noisy bus depot was our first real cultural experience. Even at that late hour it was teeming with people, all carrying soft bags and most holding young children. We stood out as foreigners in every way. Our white skin and Western clothes signaled to every man and boy selling their wares that we were potential customers with an interest in buying what they had to offer. Everything—from Kleenex to perfume to monkeys—was available for purchase. The food smells were intoxicating and inviting, but we had been warned to stay away from most street foods. I settled for a bottle of water and something that I thought were pretzels. A dozen of us huddled together in a self-protected circle and watched the entertaining commotion, which prepared us somewhat for what we would witness in Istanbul.

The trip proved to be an early lesson in the dangers of Turkish driving. Road accidents are the greatest cause of death in the country, and I now understood why we traveled in the middle of the night. School officials may have hoped we would be so exhausted from our flight that we would sleep through the night, unaware of the many close calls that would present themselves. I witnessed a few of these near misses as horns honked, brakes slammed, and headlights flashed. I drifted back to sleep with the hope I had been hallucinating. That was the last trip via bus to Istanbul. Fly, or stay home, is the more accepted and prudent mode.

Merhaba! (hello) *Hoşgeldiniz*! (welcome) *Türkiye*! (Turkey). These would become new words that would be part of my daily conversations.

Our orientation, both in Izmir and Istanbul, was a full-blown vacation. We were up early and late to bed. Our days were full of cultural orientation, language lessons, sightseeing, samplings of exotic Turkish food, and acquainting ourselves with our fellow expatriates. We were too busy to be homesick and were having too much fun to be lonely.

ORIENTATION: PREPARATION TO BE TURKIFIED

Our comfortable hotel had spectacular views and a secluded balcony. I felt rested and began to sense that learning Turkish, which we had now been exposed to in our language classes, would be easier than I'd anticipated. This, of course, turned out not to be true. Memorizing words came easy to me, but I never mastered the ability to speak in sentences. On the other hand, the knowledge we gathered concerning the history, economics, and culture of Turkey was instructive.

To know Turkish history is to become familiar with the name Atatürk. Though no longer living, his picture is displayed in every government office, in schools, and in homes. To further honor the man, large banners hang conspicuously on the outside of buildings throughout the country. Mustafa Kemal Atatürk created a new Turkey and did as much for his country as any leader in modern history. Proof of his legacy is the complete transformation of modern Turkey. He gained early recognition as a military commander, who led his charges against the invading allied forces in World War I. Later he became a national hero when his forces defeated the Greek army, including a major battle in Izmir. This prominence led to political victory when he became president of Turkey in 1923. He decided—no demanded—that Turkey abandon their feudal ways and become more Westernized. He was an advocate for women's rights including voting privileges, the banning of veils, and the right to hold office. His other accomplishments consist of secularization of the government and the establishment of the army as the guardian of this entity. This position has created a paradox for modern Turkey, while it attempts to join the European Market and gain acceptance from its brothers and sisters in Islam. The European Union looks with some fear at the Turkish army's power, and the Muslim world is alienated by their secularism. More references regarding Atatürk will follow, but this man left his mark on everything from the type of clothes people wear to the language they speak.

The view from our hotel balcony overlooking the Sea of Marmara in Istanbul provided more than the calm and picturesque sights of a busy waterway. In that chaotic city of thirteen million, the sounds of people and their playthings permeated the air. Turks loved their horns. Truck drivers in particular showed their musical tastes with the catchy melodies of their horns. The horn's primary purpose was to call attention to the car's presence and serve as a protector for the masses in and around the street. Amid the noise, the Call to Prayer soon became a haunting but welcome relief, for it represented rest, silence, and repose. Though not many stopped, the thought was planted.

Istanbul is surely one of the world's most fascinating cities. One of the highlights of our trip was our faculty ferry cruise down the Bosphorus, which is the body of water dividing the European and Asian shores of the city. Boating between Europe and Asia, we witnessed over one hundred ships from around the world waiting patiently to enter the port. The story goes that years ago a ship captain grounded his ship loaded with sheep. The ship sank and thousands of sheep floated about for weeks. Since that incident, only a Turkish captain is permitted to pilot a ship into the harbor and thus the wait may take several days! Floating up and down the strait that connects the Black Sea and the Sea of Marmara allowed us to see the Blue Mosque, Hagia Sophia, and Tokapi Palace, all considered among the most impressive churches, palaces, and museums in the world.

While our boat trip was unforgettable, the best entertainment value may have been watching the passersby on the street. Although initially disconcerting, the congestion gradually became more comforting than scary. Among the mass of people we always felt safe, which probably produced a false sense of security. With all the jostling and thrust of people moving you along, you could be robbed and not even know it. And yet, in our two years, we were never victims and we never felt personally threatened.

The Topkapi Palace, the Hagia Sophia, and the Blue Mosque are located near each other inside the old city of Istanbul. A tourist can spend two to three days on a loop of these magnificent structures. The Topkapi Palace, built in 1453, was the residence of the Sultans for almost three centuries. A full day is required to see this massive structure, with the Harem tour a must-see. To indicate its size, four hundred to five hundred people lived in the Harem quarters alone.

To restore the greatness of the Roman Empire, the Hagia Sophia was completed in 548 A.D. St. Peter's in Rome is larger than the Hagia Sophia, but it was built more than 1,000 years later. From a historical perspective, the Hagia Sophia was first built as a church, transformed into a mosque, and then proclaimed a museum by Atatürk in 1935.

The Blue Mosque is another architectural marvel built between 1606 and 1616, although it is not considered as great a triumph as the Hagia Sophia. The "blue" of the mosque's name comes from the tiles, which line the walls. It's both a tourist attraction and a place for Muslims to worship, with the five-time daily prayers a reminder to do just that.

Another highlight was our trip to the Covered Market (Grand Bazaar), located in the middle of the busy and disorganized streets of Istanbul. I was caught up in a sea of people, trying to observe the sights and not lose our guide in the dense crowd. Uncertain where we were specifically, it was exciting to think that we were in Europe, or was it Asia? At six feet five inches, looming high above the multitudes of people, I saw a familiar landmark and excitedly informed everyone of a McDonald's up ahead. I must have been a huge disappointment to our veteran guide as I asked him to stop. I had been out of America for only a few days, I was in one of the most exotic cities in the world, and I was absolutely thrilled by a McDonald's restaurant. That was shameful. But still, I strolled along, enjoying my chocolate ice cream cone.

Signs appeared that we were nearing the Market. We all stopped to receive instructions from our guide when I spotted a young man wearing a maroon and gold University of Minnesota T-shirt. Eagerly I ran up to him and called aloud, "Go Gophers!" He continued walking, looking straight ahead as though I were invisible. Assuming he had not heard me, I yelled, "University of Minnesota" a couple of times to no avail. I was distraught and, without a doubt, had brought new shame to myself. As I caught up to my group, several gave me a puzzled glance and a shake of the head. Two of the detractors looked very familiar.

We finally arrived in front of the Grand Bazaar, a maze of 4,000 shops, 58 streets, and approximately 325,000 visitors daily. I thought of it as an ancient forerunner to the Mall of America. The hustlers aggressively marketed their wares ranging from carpets to leather to jewelry. Much of the Bazaar is sectioned off by the products sold. If you want plumbing materials, just find the right area. If it's jewelry you want, there are hundreds of small shops clustered to serve you. Bargaining was expected and proved to be fun, though I was more interested in looking around than in buying. The only troubling thought was finding the designated meeting location. The network of small shops, plus numerous lane twists and turns, could quickly disorient even the most skilled navigator.

At an evening gathering at Bosphorus University, I had stimulating conversations with teachers from our sister schools. If we were back in the States, I may have taken the position of elder statesmen with the younger teachers. Yet here, regardless of their young age or lack of seniority, I had much to learn from those who had taught in Japan, Malaysia, and Northern Africa. My thirty-plus years of teaching was somewhat negated, but I didn't mind.

Our final orientation event was a dinner at the home of a foundation administrator that ran all three ACI sister schools. His apartment sat high on a cliff overlooking the Bosphorus, with Istanbul's charming hotels and government buildings looming over the waterway. It was a setting made for morning breakfasts, dinner parties, evening reflections, and repose. Life was good in Istanbul. That evening answered my question as to why someone might want to leave the comforts of the United States and live permanently in Turkey.

For a public school teacher who was used to orientations that welcomed you with a picnic of beans and hot dogs, and perhaps a look at the lay of the land from the back of a school bus, this was authentic red-carpet treatment. We didn't have time to be lonesome and fearful, only time to enjoy being hosted in a most gracious, generous, and thoughtful manner.

After four extraordinary days, the Istanbul orientation ended, and we traveled back to Izmir. There we continued an in-depth tour of our newly adopted city. As I previously mentioned, Izmir is located on the Aegean Sea with mountains as the backdrop. The setting has great potential, though it may never be realized because of its polluted harbor and the starkness of its architecture. The boxy looking apartments, covered with eight stories of concrete, have detracted from the harbor's beauty, along with the aforementioned damage that major fires, earthquakes, and wars can pass on. Yet, I would forever appreciate and enjoy the natural physical beauty.

Of Izmir's three million people, I don't believe I met one who didn't treat me well. Sales people, fellow workers, taxi drivers, students, school staff, apartment dwellers, and those I passed on the street all fit into that description. The Turks proved to be helpful, caring, and genuinely sincere in their efforts. The exceptions were drivers who seemed to be on a mission to hit pedestrians—either native or foreign.

Each new foreign family was assigned a host family. We were most fortunate. Belma, a biology teacher, and her family invited us to their summer home in Çeşme, an hour from the city. Çeşme is the summer haven for people from Izmir who love the sea, the cooler breezes, and the relative quiet. Belma loved to cook, eat, talk, and swim. We did all in good order. So, soon after returning from Istanbul, tired and a bit overwhelmed, we were on our way to Çeşme to enjoy our host family's hospitality. As they had gone ahead of us, we made our first solo attempt at taking a bus. We survived two bus transfers and a taxi ride to reach Belma's home, a comfortable cottage located two blocks from the sea. During our stay in Turkey, we were fortunate to spend three delightful weekends as her guests in Çeşme.

Orientation continued at a high pace for all of us. Turkish historians and teachers taught us the historical, economic, and political reality of Turkey. I was eager to learn and absorb my newfound knowledge and wondered why I hadn't felt this passion for learning during my years of school. It was easy to embrace the whole experience.

But how much did I want to change? Would I become ensconced in Turkish life? I tried not to get too high or too low regarding my feelings about my new situation, but most days I was pretty puffed up about being there. The change and stimulation were dramatic, which energized me. When I calmed down, I would remind myself that this was not the norm. This was an orientation where we were not only educated, but also entertained, flattered, and otherwise kept busy. These two weeks would not prepare us for all the struggles that would lie ahead, but it was a novel and relaxing diversion.

Striking Out On Our Own

After two weeks of being pampered and herded through a regimented orientation, two families made the decision to eat out on our own. The outcome indicated that we weren't ready. We ordered what we thought would be vegetarian pizza, but it was covered with lamb; and our "grilled cheese" was neither grilled nor did it have cheese. Our problems continued to mount when we received our bill and had to call the waiter over to explain it to us. We huddled together (we have pictures) to come up with the correct amount, and we left the restaurant with the satisfaction that comes only with success. As we walked smartly down the street, we heard the waiter calling out to us and turned to see the owner waving the bill. They gestured that we had underpaid, so we meekly returned to the restaurant to huddle up once again. Confusion reigned, but we paid another 250,000 lira ($3.00). We were certain that we had been taken advantage of and made a pact not to return. We also decided that from now on we'd make our own grilled cheese (with cheese) and our own vegetarian pizza (without meat).

Maybe drivers weren't the only ones who had it in for us—this restaurant owner could be added to the list.

FIRST HALF

American missionaries founded The American Collegiate Institute (ACI) 120 years ago. Today the school is secular and is run by a private foundation formed by the graduates of ACI and its sister schools in Istanbul and Tarsus. The school's name is indicative of a curriculum that emphasizes English classes and American-style, extra-curricular activities. ACI graduates are accepted in schools around the world and, in particular, the United States, Canada, and the United Kingdom. In addition, we found that the Turkish Ministry and its instructional dictates are clearly a part of any educational program in Turkey.

My position at ACI was to be a teacher, Physical Education Department chair, athletic director, and basketball coach. There were five people in our department—three Turks, Kivanç Hanim, Figen Hanim, and Sahlattin Bey (*Hanim* indicates "Mrs./Ms." and *Bey* designates "Mr."); one Canadian, Jackie; and myself. One person was bilingual, two spoke only Turkish, and two spoke only English. My goal was to take a team-oriented approach to teaching that would require us to be cohesive and cooperative. That included everything from scheduling classes, facility use, and team-teaching specified classes. We would work together and, hopefully, enjoy the experience. With our language issues, we would not bore each other with unnecessary talk, long meetings, gossip, and chitchat!

SCHOOL DAYS

One thousand Turks from grades 6–12 populated the school. The breakdown by grade:

Prep, 6th grade	Lise 1, 10th grade
Orta 1, 7th grade	Lise 2, 11th grade
Orta 2, 8th grade	Lise 3, 12th grade
Orta 3, 9th grade	

The student body of 144 was selected each year from approximately 1,300 children who took an entrance exam for which they'd been tutored and had studied very hard. We had the chance to proctor the exams one weekend during our first year when prospective students flooded the campus accompanied by their anxiety-ridden parents. The dark-eyed, ever alert, eleven-year-old mini-Turks were armed for the task with a handful of aids—bottled water, pencils, erasers, and a healthy dose of confidence bolstered by a solid year of preparation. The students plowed through one hundred multiple choice questions, which had been prepared in seclusion by three Turkish scholars. The parents fidgeted outside, smoked, and worried throughout the morning. The exam was a big deal; a child's life could be altered. We were impressed by the children's sense of purpose as they approached the test, much like young professional accountants taking an impending CPA exam. The pressure on young Turkish students concerning their academics was enormous. The select 144 students would be notified of their acceptance, and the unlucky 1,156 would either test at another private school or enroll in a government school.

These incoming Prep students did not speak English, but were immersed in the language from day one. After a very short time, the new students were able to greet their teachers by saying, "How are you today? I am fine, thank you." They both asked and answered their own greeting.

My first impression of the students was that they were well dressed. The boys wore white shirts, navy blazers, gray slacks, and ties. The girls wore plaid skirts, white blouses, and matching knee-highs. Most of us agreed it was a nice change from the accepted dress at the majority of American schools. On special occasions—the first day of school for example—the girls wore their more formal attire, which consisted of their normal uniform plus a navy blazer and pantyhose. (Jennifer thought the casual uniform a great idea and was delighted that she could use her Scottish kilt pin to secure her plaid skirt. However, every day that she was obliged to wear her blazer and the dreaded pantyhose, she would unfailingly return to our apartment with a burgeoning stomachache.)

The students were enthusiastic and never hesitated to volunteer or raise their hand. They were also very curious, social, and loved to chat—without reservation. Noticeably attractive with the blending of their dark eyes, black hair, and olive skin, they were polite to each other and respectful to teachers to the point that they stood as one when we entered the classroom. That was a bit of a shock; the flattery took some getting used to.

Although I enjoyed teaching all grades, I especially got a kick out of the Prep students. True, there were frustrations galore, but the humorous side almost always prevailed. Early in the year, for instance, I remember peeking into the Prep class dressing room to see a husky Prep student standing quietly by as another boy dressed him. Everyone else was occupied with their needs, so I stopped to watch as his friend finished buttoning his shirt and attempted to fix his tie. My first thought was that student must have been blind. As I later learned, however, he was the product of a too-often-typical Turkish mother who, until then, had helped her son get dressed. I would continue to observe the helpful nature of Turks expressed both in and out of school.

The bright red sweaters that the Prep students wore secured for them the nickname, "The Tomatoes." They moved about the campus in groups and one could see "The Tomatoes" clearly as they hustled from class to class, trying very hard to be on time as they too tended to be chatty. To ensure that they were dressed properly when they left our physical education class, we had an informal uniform check to be certain that everything was hooked up, tucked in, and belted together. On one particular day, the students lined up casually outside my office, still red-faced and perspiring from our activity. I zeroed in on Yiğit (pronounced "Yeet"), the student who had been earlier assisted in his dress. There he was, proudly displaying himself. He looked good. His hair was damp but neatly parted. His collar was askew, but the tie was in place. I noticed a catsup stain on his shirt, but so far so good. His pants were tight, probably last year's purchase, and the belt was under tremendous strain. Checking further, I saw yet another food stain, and finally found an undeniable reason for continued inspection. Yiğit's white shirt was staring at me from the opening in his unzipped pants. As we were not yet on English-speaking terms, I pointed, he tucked, he zipped, and then proudly strutted off to his next class.

Teachers

The Turkish teachers at first glance appeared to be quite serious and professional. And they too were well-dressed compared to their American counterparts. The Turkish men took pride in their sharply cut European suits. Ties and dress shirts were worn daily. There were also several who managed to sneak in an old tweed coat from the '60s, which in my opinion complimented their professional look.

The women were not dressed as we had seen in pictures. Before leaving for Turkey, we had read books that suggested women dress in closed-toe shoes and long-sleeved shapeless dresses that were modest in length. We were shocked the first day of school to see some of the younger Turkish teachers wearing short, black, leather skirts, sleeveless tops, and ample makeup. These teachers definitely presented a challenge to the foreign staff to upgrade their dress a level or two.

Campus

The school itself was an oasis in the dry, dusty environment of Göztepe, the section of Izmir where we lived and worked. The eleven-acre campus, enclosed by a brick wall and guarded at three entries around the clock, was located on a steep hill. Scattered among the buildings were dozens of olive trees and ever-blooming flowers of countless varieties. The buildings were randomly situated in the garden-like setting, a haven from the noise and pollution of the neighborhood and street. To reach the classroom buildings, we were forced to manage hundreds of steps, which constituted a healthy morning workout.

The campus could be a quiet reprieve or a boisterous playground, depending on the event. On Monday mornings, the amphitheater, located in the heart of the campus, was the focal point. The raising of the Turkish flag was always impressive and solemn as the well-clad students stood at attention, each with their arms clinging tightly to their sides and their eyes fixed straight ahead. This ceremony contrasted with the noontime soccer games, when balls flew amid the sound of a Western rock song blaring from a well-placed speaker. The Turks liked action and were comfortable with clattering noise as a goal was scored or a three-point shot swished through the net. A familiar chant often accompanied a winning shot or game.

Grading Philosophy

The school's philosophy on grading was vastly different from that of American schools. Normally this would not concern me, but as Jennifer was a student at ACI during her last two years of high school, this philosophical difference could become a problem when she prepared to enter an American university. The Turkish system emphasized the exam and classroom participation and placed less value on daily assignments. Classroom participation at times posed a problem for Jennifer, for the students often reverted to their own Turkish language when they needed to more clearly express themselves.

Every student graduate was subjected to the University Exam to gain acceptance into a limited number of colleges. This exam drove the students' lives from grades 10–12, often including additional lessons from tutors after the regular school day. Students also attended what was known as *Derşane* (cram school) on weekends. Although the school had an excellent curriculum in math and science, extra lessons were deemed necessary to guarantee better test scores in these subjects. As a result, the extra preparations caused most, if not all, senior students to drop out of their extra-curricular activities. Jennifer didn't have the advantage of taking cram classes and, therefore, relied on a math tutor and additional preparation on her own.

Starting Out

On my first day of school, I faced 24 twelve-year-old Prep students all wearing blue shorts and white T-shirts, ready to participate. They looked eager to learn and had a confident air about them. To say that they appeared ready was an understatement. I was fifty-nine years old with years of experience, and I was scared. I spoke virtually no Turkish and they spoke no English. Where would we start? How would I teach games to students who didn't speak English? How would I give directions? I had an idea and a plan, but would it work? I took attendance and found myself struggling to pronounce names like Yiğit, Serhat, and Kivanç. They listened respectfully and, when the giggling stopped, corrected me. It took ten minutes to place them in six rows of four students each.

I took a deep breath and reminded myself that I had traveled thousands of miles to teach English to Turkish students. I pointed at my eyes and with hand gestures said, "You, watch me." I held up my arm and said the word "arm." Then I motioned to them to hold up their arm and repeat the word in English. Learning our body parts—arm, leg, shoulder, head, neck—was our first lesson. Once the word was learned, we practiced moving or exercising that body part. Modeling a movement and having them repeat the behavior was my teaching technique—hopping on one leg, jumping on two, waving an arm. The lesson went well and provided me with a few chuckles and many smiles.

The second week, we learned the words for directions and for a variety of movements. The kids hopped backward, slid laterally, and skipped forward. Generally, I found the students lacking in fundamental movement skills and out of condition. In plain language, they were uncoordinated. The movement activities gave them the exercise they needed, while their communication and athletic skills would come later. I gave the English teachers the words we learned in class, which they included with the vocabulary they taught. This quickened the learning and made English class more relevant.

Teaching proved to be hard work, and by Friday I was fatigued. I found the energy level needed to teach physical education to energetic youngsters draining. In addition, the physical demands that were required daily to haul equipment between the storage facilities and the courts, while moving up and down hills, was exhausting. My legs were sore and tired and, by week's end, I was moving down the endless steps sideways to ease the pain. I was one tired puppy!

Though I was often tired, I initially relished my students' enthusiasm for chanting. With little encouragement, Turkish folk of all ages broke into a litany of rhythmic words. As I was addressing my non-English-speaking Prep class one day, I complimented them with the ultimate accolade, "*Çok güzel*" (very beautiful or good job). First of all, they were pleased because I had spoken Turkish, which we were discouraged from doing; and secondly, I had paid them a compliment. Not able to contain themselves, they chanted in unison, "Mis-ter John-son," clap, clap, clap-clap-clap, "Mis-ter John-son," clap, clap, clap-clap-clap.

Getting swept up in the moment, I created an animated dance, timing my steps to the beat of their voices and the clap of their hands. This made them shout louder and clap harder. I continued to dance, adding a pirouette along with some elaborate arm movements. My body was turning—no spinning—with the beat. I began to clap with my hands held high, heeling and toeing, knees lifted in sync, encouraging the students to join me. This spectacle took place on the outdoor court below the windows of the Science Hall. Students from the classrooms began to poke their heads out the windows. Slowly the chant and the beat of the movement swept through their classrooms. Now we had a chorus of voices led by my chant-hungry Prep class, joined in by middle school science students and choreographed by their hambone teacher. What we produced was a true combination of discordant sounds and a medley of missteps. Needless to say, it was fun!

Bargaining for Equipment the Turkish Way

ACI was anxious to get a new gym. Our school director, Dr. Thompson, Turkish physical education teacher and translator, Kivanç Hanim, and I went to visit a new school in Izmir for ideas. Their gymnasium was large but not practical for the multiple uses we had in mind. It was great for indoor soccer, but would not meet the needs of a full-fledged physical education program. ACI offered a curriculum that paralleled American education, with classes that specified unusual court markings for games (for example pickle ball) unique to America but not to Turkey. We would need a weight training room, a combination exercise room/dance room, and a facility that could house several different activities simultaneously.

Because of our unique needs, it was decided that the school's business manager and I would visit three Turkish schools in Istanbul that used a similar American curriculum. We flew up for the day. The visit proved worthwhile for him to see the kind of gym I was proposing. Our school was serious about the project, and our ideas could now be presented to the architect.

An afternoon was devoted to purchasing athletic equipment for class and sports. I needed a translator, so Ahmet Bey, the school's building and grounds manager, and I went to Alsancak to buy (a.k.a. bargain) equipment for the year.

A short, dark-haired, brown-eyed man of boundless energy, Ahmet Bey could speak in Turkish on his ever-present cell phone while carrying on a meaningful conversation with me in English. He was responsible for approximately fifty workers and dozens of buildings. He was also the designated mediator between the foreign teachers and Turkish culture. He helped us with pass-ports, telephones, housing problems, and furniture requests, and listened to daily complaints from lonely and whiny foreigners. He was the foreign teachers' stabling influence as we fretted about everything. His job was unthinkable, never ending, and impossible. "Yes, I can do that, Mr. Craig," was his routine response to a request. He was so good at his job that he could convince you that he would do something that we both knew was unlikely to occur.

Ahmet Bey knew various retailers and loved the give-and-take of the Turkish economic system. Our shopping spree went something like this: we entered a store expressing a desire to buy equipment and asked for the best price they could offer. The store compiled a list of the equipment and their prices. Then we were off to the next store to repeat the same mantra. All the while, Ahmet Bey was negotiating fiercely, using the skill he honed through his many years as a purchasing agent in the Turkish military. The two of us would converse in English during this process. Ahmet would say things to me like, "We can do better than this at the next store," or "I know the owner down the street," and, finally, the real coup d'etat, "We'll go last to the biggest store in Izmir, Barçin Spor. The owner's grandson goes to ACI and he must give us the best price." He was determined as he repeated, "He must."

This conversation, of course, took place in front of the store-owners in English. It was kind of fun, but I also felt guilty. As far as I could tell, we had no intention of buying from them.

Finally, we arrived at Barçin Spor and settled down to a glass of tea. Ahmet began the bargaining as he passed the list of equipment needs across the desk. On the list were the best prices of the previously visited companies. There was a heated, or at least animated, exchange of words. Finally, the owners decided they would look everything over and fax us their prices.

Four hours after we began this search for bargain prices, we headed back to ACI by taxi. Our driver had earlier returned to ACI to do some of the many errands that Ahmet Bey had assigned him. None of the workers were allowed to make many decisions without Ahmet Bey's input. Everything had to be approved by him, hence the ever-present, always-ringing cell phone.

He assured me again that Barçin Spor would come through with the best price because of the owner's grandson being a student at ACI. Later the prices were faxed to us. I was given a copy to apply to my budget and was assured that the prices were heavily discounted. Only in Turkey!

Our Family Reunites

In late October, the rest of our family arrived in Turkey. Our oldest son, Craig, and his girlfriend, Heidi, joined our second son, Kurt, in Istanbul. Craig and Heidi were in transit from

Chicago and Kurt from his Peace Corps post in Nepal. They spent a couple of days in Istanbul taking in the sounds and sights before flying to Izmir. We watched from the balcony window as they arrived by taxi at 9:15 in the evening. Kurt hung out the front passenger window flashing the peace sign. What a pleasure it was to have our whole family with us to share in this cultural and transforming experience in Turkey!

We visited late into the night. I found myself listening and watching for signs of changes in each of us. Three of us had been in Turkey almost three months, and Kurt had been in Nepal for about a year. The setting of our bare-bones apartment in Izmir, surrounded by Ottoman mystique and Muslim culture, somehow made this reunion much more dramatic and meaningful.

Craig, Heidi, and Kurt spent their days sightseeing, while we were in school. On nights and weekends we took off in search of a ruin or a carpet. Izmir was our base and we found both informal and entertaining activities; we all came to know a bit more about the country and maybe about ourselves in the process.

Some of our highlights were our visit to Ephesus, buying carpets at Roza's, and dinner at Asansor's—a restaurant high above the city streets that provided a wonderful view. The two weeks went much too quickly, and before we had even made a nick in our many plans, Craig and Heidi were set to leave. There was talk of a marriage between Craig and Heidi, but nothing definite. We were not planning on coming home for the summer, but for a wedding we would make an exception. It was great getting to know Heidi better; our family would happily welcome a thoughtful and gracious daughter-in-law. Kurt stayed a few weeks longer before returning to Nepal, where he worked at a fish farm. The concept of teaching farmers how to raise fish to supplement their meager income was a good one, but according to Kurt's early analysis, results would take time.

It was difficult to assess what the boys and Heidi truly felt about our living arrangement and circumstances in Turkey. We were sure that their feelings were mixed, and yet they seemed to take in stride our lack of air conditioning, daily shortage of water, and humble surroundings. As they drove off in the taxi on their way back to the airport, they were probably concerned about leaving us, but also proud that we seemed to be living success-fully in an unmistakably foreign land.

Kicking Back

A sunny seventy-five-degree day, accompanied by a breeze from the nearby Aegean Sea, made for near perfect weather. I was seated on a bench overlooking the campus, a setting that allowed me a view of countless ripened olive trees. Numerous roses were blooming and splendid in the noonday sun. Here and there, workers were sweeping (always sweeping), trimming, shaping, and grooming one of the few lush areas in all of Izmir.

A far off ferryboat caught my eye as it crossed the harbor on its hourly cruise. It bobbed and wove its way around buoys and boats, much the way my students dribbled a soccer ball through a sea of cones to practice their skills . . . always keeping their destination in mind, but never able to take the shortest distance.

Students enjoyed free play on the courts. Soccer, ah yes, always soccer in Turkey. They played dressed in their formal wear: white shirts, ties, and court shoes. Their black hair was matted to their heads with sweat, and the now wrinkled white dress shirts gradually worked their way out of their trousers. Students began each day looking neat and clean and, at the end of the day, they left campus looking much like miniature busi-nessmen who had stopped to fix a flat tire.

I studied the age-old amphitheater, a setting where we started and ended each week with the traditional flag ceremony. A well-worn copy of earlier times, this venerable theater was also well-utilized. Scattered about the concrete structure laced with wooden benches were students sunning and enjoying a brief respite from the rigors of school.

Indeed, students were always everywhere. Walking, talking,

eating—hardly anyone was alone. Due to their social nature, the students were involved; no one was discounted. Some sat on benches in small, secluded enclaves of flowers and trees. A number stood draped over the recessed athletic courts, clinging to the fence that separated them from the action. Even though they weren't playing, their cheering and chanting included them in the competition.

All these observations during a lunch break—another slice of Turkey!

The campus environment was so much less institutional than any school I had known and, as a result, became a more pleasant place to teach. The setting was a fringe benefit that I valued so much that, at various times while working, it didn't seem like work. This non-work attitude is a wonderful feeling and one that I experienced often in my early teaching years. As it's been said, "Find a job that you love, and you'll never work a day in your life."

After that particular day of work and personal lunchtime reflection, the staff and teachers were invited to Turkish Night, a celebration held in the amphitheater. The Turks knew how to party. Folk dancing was the highlight. The women danced and whirled in colorful Turkish costumes with loose fitting skirts and peasant-like blouses. They moved with a light step and a practiced grace. Turks love to perform, and they do it well. The high-stepping routine of the men required physical strength, discipline, and a stoic presence. They jumped, stomped, and kicked with precise movement. Turkish men and women used their arms and hands. Arms, fully extended, with a slight bend at the elbow meant the fingers were always poised to snap to the beat. I took to it naturally. Of course, that is just an opinion. (Maybe there is a bit of Turk in this Scandinavian/Scottish body.)

We ate Turkish cuisine, smoked a water pipe, danced, and even attempted to sing a Turkish song or two. The evening took a dramatic turn when the person in charge of music played old-fashioned American rock for our pleasure. We welcomed the familiar sound, but, in retrospect, the Turks may not have appreciated Western rock music on Turkish night.

Many hours earlier we had been skeptical, excited, and curious about Turkish night. Five hours later a weary crew of foreigners walked home. The evening suggested that our new friends were beginning to accept us. There would be expectations of us as the Turks invited us into their culture. We hoped we had begun the process of measuring up to those expectations, for we were truly beginning to appreciate both our new friends and their culture.

Oh That Enthusiasm . . .

You're standing in front of the class. You have posed a question and hands have flown up—not just one, but most. Every time! Moreover, students willingly volunteer to help with equipment, apologize profusely when reprimanded, and are always enthusiastic to the point of being hyperactive. Most of my disciplinary action was necessitated by this enthusiasm, which needed to be contained at times. The students weren't perfect, but the problems they presented were usually a result of their inquisitive nature and subsequent outgoing behavior. Remember, the students had passed rigorous tests to enter this school; they were all smart.

One particular highlight took place early in the school year. We were again working on names of body parts and movement skills. Spontaneously, I instructed the twenty-four Prep students to join hands and form a circle. Language barriers persisted, so this formation took about ten minutes. The Hokey Pokey was made for this situation. Without music and having forgotten some of the words, or at least the sequence, I began to sing and demonstrate the song with my movements. I started with the phrase, "Put your left arm in, put your left arm out, put your left arm in, and shake it all about." The students joined in and we worked our way up and down the body parts, ad-libbing when necessary. We ended the song with "shake it all about," as the excitable Turks were approaching frenzy. Luckily, no one was injured.

The students loved the dance and naturally wanted more. Fortunately, the class time had elapsed and the class ended with a chant, "Mis-ter John-son, Mis-ter John-son," clap, clap, clap-clap-clap. I sashayed off the court to the beat of the chant, with knees hurting, and dripping in sweat, telling myself that I love this job. The word spread and the Hokey Pokey became a part of every Prep class routine.

Not all times were as smooth as the Hokey Pokey class, however. The following is an example of how tenuous my hold was on my students. I had just finished a demonstration on how to shoot a basketball, without holding a ball. I showed the proper position of the hand, elbow, and feet. Next the class practiced the shadow shooting model, again without a ball. Then I instructed all of them to sit down, which is a critical command when teaching young kids. The class was now seated in four rows on each side of me, and I asked the first person in each row to stand up, walk to the bag of balls, and get one. The second student in one line, either not listening or unable to understand, saw four students running to get a ball. His thought must have been, "I'm missing out." He broke ranks and ran to the balls. Suddenly, a chain reaction occurred. Every child in class was now up and headed for the bag of balls. They dived in head first, swarming like sweet ants after a piece of sugar. As soon as they came up for air, smiling and holding a ball, they quickly ran for the nearest basket.

Seconds earlier, we had a controlled learning situation. Now we had chaos. Balls were flying, students were running in every direction, and I attempted to stand my ground in their midst, dazed and perplexed. It was wild, crazy, funny, and an example of how delicate the balance is between teacher control and pandemonium. I had to rethink my teaching strategy for the next class. It would be my fault if it happened again.

One fall day, a theater group from England performed at our school. The group presented a variety of skits and songs that required audience participation. When one presenter asked for volunteers, the ever-willing young Turks literally jumped out of their seats to gain his attention. I have mentioned that they were always willing and eager to respond in the classroom, but this surprised me. Having sat through countless lyceums over the years watching most American kids shrink down in their seats in fear, this was interesting. If there is such a thing as a performance gene, the Turks possess it in good supply. I also noticed that once they were selected to talk, sing, and even dance in front of their peers, they were poised and very comfortable with themselves. Did these kids represent the norm of Turkey?

Student life wasn't always perfect in Turkey, however. My first incident occurred when I became very angry with my class, as they were disrespectful to each other and to me. If this had happened back in the States, I would have yelled and scolded my class. Well, I must have been getting acclimated as I did the same thing in this situation. The kids were shocked. They couldn't believe that their buddy, Mr. Johnson, would get upset with them.

The problem centered on their listening skills, which in a second language situation is essential for comprehension. Their vocabulary was so minimal that I had to speak clearly and use words that they understood. If I didn't, I would lose them. In fact, even if I did speak clearly, I sometimes lost them. So it would seem that I, too, was part of the problem. While we talked it through, I still think I shook up my little friends and provided some conversation at dinner time when the inevitable question, "How was school today?" was asked.

We were also having some problems within our staff. Selfishness was evident and cooperation was lacking as we struggled to schedule gym time for team practices and classes. Two of the Turks were set in their ways and seemed unwilling to compromise. Since our limited space demanded conciliation, I volunteered to practice basketball on the outside courts to ease the tension. The fact that the outside courts were regulation size made my decision easy. The court's new surface and the good, solid rims were also a factor. As for the gym, it had crooked rims, the floor was pocked with dead spots, and the walls butted up against the out-of-bounds line. The one advantage of the gym was that it had a roof, though negated somewhat by the eleven spots that leaked. (This is fact because I often placed the buckets around the gym when there was a significant rainfall.)

Educating and Being Educated

One weekend, department heads—like myself—attended a planning workshop on curriculum and philosophy at a seaside resort, an hour's drive from Izmir. The group worked intensely, and I was impressed. I felt fortunate to observe the school leaders think, plan, and respond to each other and to the different ideas that were posed. They took this planning session seriously. When I began teaching in Turkey, I felt very much like an outsider who was merely visiting for a couple of years. But as time went on, I began to feel a personal and professional commitment to the hardworking teachers and students.

My undocumented but well-thought-out goal was that while in Turkey, I would work hard for the students, relish the adventure, and try not to get entangled in school politics. Up until that point, mission accomplished. However, I began to sense some weakening on my decision not to get involved.

The presence of the Turkish Ministry was considerable. Even Turks agreed that their policies were out of touch. Nevertheless, their rules were set and we had no choice but to follow them. The Turks' response regarding the Ministry was not unlike American teachers' attitudes toward our Education Department. The difference was that the Turkish teachers, and their culture in general, were more compliant. Our culture promotes the love of freedom and advocacy of rights, whereas

Turkey has a high level of authoritarianism and fear of the law.

As department head, I had a responsibility to the Ministry, but disagreed vehemently with much of their educational philosophy. It was apparent that some factions in the school embraced change, while others were more traditional in their belief. The role of the foreign faculty had not been clearly defined other than an orientation phrase that struck me: "Just eat the grapes, don't fight the battles." Thus, I questioned how hard I should push for change, and what changes I should advocate. I was trying to be sensitive to their traditions and refused to be the "ugly American" I had read about.

A comprehensive curriculum is particularly critical for international schools because of continual staff turnover. In my past experience, however, curriculum guides were often found hidden high on a dusty shelf. Curriculum guides—if written relevantly and with the needs of the students in mind—should be on one's desk, open for daily reference for assessment, coordination, and planning. We were assigned to develop a new curriculum for the department, and we hoped what we wrote (and adopted from Wayzata, Minnesota's school system) would be just such a useful and viable instrument for ACI.

The importance of weekly department meetings existed because of our mutual language and communication difficulties. Many days, the extent of our office interaction would be to greet each other with "*merhaba*" (hello) and "*nasilsiniz*" (how are you?). To inquire about their class, or if there were any problems, was totally out of the question. I came in many mornings anxious to share an experience, and all I could do was smile and feebly greet them.

When I did attempt to converse with one of my colleagues, my inadequate Turkish led me to frustration and a gesture that said, "We'll talk later." We each had memorized a few scripted words in English or Turkish, but more often than not we would wait for Kivanç, our bilingual department member, to resolve our quandary. At times, even Kivanç was bewildered, which led me to wonder about the validity of past translations.

What's the Point? Teach to the Objective

An announcement was made that the department heads were to receive staff development training from the United States in order to upgrade their programs and improve the classroom instruction. This was interesting to me because I had been a staff development trainer for Wayzata from 1985–1991. The trainer for our session was Carol Cummings. I had participated in her workshops in Minneapolis and Seattle in the late 1980s. She would deliver a four-day workshop for department heads and selected staff. She was a good model for teaching strategies, and I felt comfortable in the workshop. I was never an expert in America and was not about to become one here; so I listened, participated, and contributed when asked. The workshop was designed to teach teachers the elements of basic instruction: how kids learn and, as a teacher, how to help kids learn.

Her workshop was basic and good stuff. As department heads, we were to learn the elements of instruction and apply that learning with teachers in our departments using observations and conferences. The first element of instruction was called "teaching to the objective," where you write an objective and then design a lesson to teach that objective. Every objective is broken down into what you want the student to learn and a behavior from the student to show that learning. To assess and apply the element of "teaching to the objective," I decided to teach an American line-dancing unit.

To prepare for the addition of an American dance unit, several things had to happen. Convincing both of the female Turkish teachers in the Physical Education Department to agree was easy as they loved to dance, even though line-dancing was not in their repertoire. Sehlattin Bey, the Turkish male teacher, was initially hesitant, but we insisted his classes participate. Soon his reluctance gave way to a cooperative spirit when the beat of the music got to his soul. CDs were ordered from an former source, Gopher Athletic Supply in Owatonna, Minnesota. This unit would prove to be a turnabout for our department because our conjoined classes forced us to plan together, communicate, and team-teach. All a first! This was a good opportunity for me to observe firsthand the talent possessed by the other teachers.

We made the decision to conduct the class in the gym for privacy and control-purposes. Our only hope was that we wouldn't lose a little Prep student falling through one of the weak spots in the floor. The old gym was packed as we grouped the three classes into lines facing a teacher. The left foot heel-toe was demonstrated, then the right foot, and so on. No music was used, and we walked them through the process. We added a pivot and a kick turn, a step behind step move (that was my favorite), and then practiced the steps over and over. The enthusiasm and energy level was high, while the listening and attentiveness was occasional.

The Turkish teachers came up with the suggestion that we would test the students on the five steps. Each student was required to perform, and they were graded accordingly. Students were used to being tested and thrived on the pressure, loved the accountability, and usually performed above what was expected. You could observe students at various times during the day performing their routine—in the cafeteria area, the outside courts, and all around the campus. Students even taught the dance steps to those not taking the class. So the unit was off to an "Achy Breaky Heart" start, which proved to be the favorite song. Go Turks! Go Billy Ray Cyrus!

Watching Turkish students perform to American music gave me a strong sense of accomplishment. The activity fed the need that every teacher has to make a difference in the lives of their students. We changed lives, not by dancing to "Achy Breaky Heart" or "Boot Scootin' Boogie," but by exposing them to new learning, making it fun, and opening their minds to the differences that existed between America and Turkey. The American

Collegiate Institute lived up to its name, as students learned both cultural differences and a new language. Everyone wanted to be a cowboy.

Picture this—the Turkish campus is sprinkled with sun-splashed, age-old olive trees surrounding a historic amphitheater. The stands are filled with a thousand students and a few hundred parents, eager to celebrate Children's Day, a national holiday. Various groups sing Turkish and American songs and a dance club performs a Turkish folk dance in full Ottoman regalia. The scene is impressive and seems to compliment the historic environment where we are all seated. But wait, the Prep physical education class is waiting in the wings. What will they perform? You got it! "Achy Breaky Heart." The uniform is a cowboy look, complete with red bandanas. The class steps and twirls, their dark heads bouncing with the beat. The song and dance become more than the thousand watching students can bear. They all rise and clap, sway and sing, accompanying the performance without exception. A standing ovation follows, led by me.

They were my students, though Figen, one of our physical education teachers, arranged the dance. It was great! Country music and line dancing may be the rage in Turkey by the time they graduate.

The Things Kids Say . . . And Do

Doğan, a Prep student, approached me in the library one day as I was talking with two older students. He had a peculiar look on his face as he drew me aside from the others.

"Mr. Johnson, you remind me of my grandfather," he said, staring up at me. My first thought was that this was a compliment. My next thought was, maybe this was a compliment I could do without. Suddenly, he grabbed me around my waist, buried his head in my side, hugged me tightly, and muffled, "And I love my grandfather!"

This was a touching example of how demonstrative and

affectionate the Turkish people are. I was the only one who appeared ill-at-ease. Doğan and I had several clashes of will during the year, and he was not a beloved student of mine. Was that why I reminded him of his grandfather? As is often the case, the non-beloved types are the students a teacher usually gets the closest to (as long as the teacher didn't lose it during the discipline process).

An example of disciplining a student and their response took place during a tennis unit. During a repetitious drilling exercise, I asked Mehmet to sit down as I didn't feel he was putting forth a good effort and, in the process, was disrupting the class. Seated off to the side, he leaned against a fence when we switched drills. When classmates passed by Mehmet, he would implore them to, "Ask Mr. Johnson if I can come back and play. Please ask him." Classmate after classmate would approach me and say, "Mr. Johnson, please let Mehmet play again. He is sorry; he didn't mean it." This went on for several minutes before I finally announced, "The next person who comes pleading to me will also sit out." That stopped the nonsense. (Coming to the aid of a fellow classmate in that type of situation was a very typical response for Turkish kids.)

I often observed parent and student interactions on campus. Turkish and American moms both share the joy of visiting their children in their schools. The similarity ends there. Turkish students loved to see their parents and often streaked toward them with outstretched arms. They typically hugged and kissed Turkish style on each cheek. An American student's response upon seeing an approaching parent in the hallway would quite likely be embarrassment and a strong desire to become invisible, or at least do a quick turn around and run for cover. I envied and respected the lack of restraint the Turks had in expressing their emotions. This was true for all ages. Students of the same sex even strolled the campus with arms entwined.

We Scandinavians were both impaired and challenged when the genes for self-expression were distributed to the Vikings of old. I hadn't hugged and kissed (on both cheeks mind you) like I did in Turkey since my crib days back in Minnesota. My Aunt Evelyn was my least favorite visiting relative, for she would always offer a full-blown hug and kiss, though I cowered in modesty. In Turkey, even real men hug and kiss. I was coming around.

The teaching unit that followed dance was gymnastics. The enthusiasm of the students prevailed, but the skill level we had observed in dancing was missing. In fact, the students' lack of spatial awareness and other skills needed to be a gymnast reminded me of my own incompetence. Some could not even do a forward roll. And the backward roll? Forget it. It required dexterity that only the advanced could handle. Maybe next year.

One of the things I enjoyed the most about teaching physical education was the special times I had with students while walking to and from class. There were many teachable moments, and I got to know the students on a whole different level. I could also practice my weak Turkish, and they could work on their rapidly flourishing English. Oh, to be young and a quick learner!

On one occasion, small, smiley Can said to me as we walked to the courts, "Mr. Johnson, I like your smile."

I smiled and offered an unassuming thank you.

He continued, "I like the way all the gold in your mouth shines."

Hey, he meant it as a compliment. I was happy to know that even though gold fillings were outmoded in most circles, they were not in Can's.

Learning the Turkish language was a slow process, and I sensed the need for a "go-to Turkish phrase" that I could memorize and use on a daily basis. While causally visiting with a student about this, he suggested that I ask the simple question, "What are you doing after school today?" This phrase would be something that was always relevant, timely, and easy to learn. What a smart kid! So my practiced conversation went like this:

"*Nasilsiniz*?" (How are you?)

"*Iyiyim, teşekkur ederim.*" (I'm fine, thank you.)

I would then casually drop, "*Okuldan sonra ne yapicaksin?*" (What are you doing after school today?)

This worked well when a couple of students responded in English, "Oh Mr. Johnson, you know Turkish very well."

In an attempt to be modest, I said, "It's not easy for me, but I'm trying."

The problems came when the student replied back in Turkish. Then I was in trouble. I learned that "*tabii tabii*" (of course, of course) would often suffice.

Jean and I commented regularly on how much we both enjoyed our jobs. We relished the flexibility, for each day's schedule was different; we appreciated the never-ending enthusiasm of the students; and we enjoyed the daily stimulation of living and teaching in Turkey. We hoped the second year would offer the same satisfaction.

CULTURE AND THE
SHOCK OF IT ALL

Adapting to new surroundings, be it a different school, job, or even a new home, can produce enough change in a person's routine to cause anxiety. Culture shock also affects self-esteem and even judgment. Occasionally, standing in front of my class, I felt inadequate or hesitant about my role with the students. One particular day, while the students were lining up for attendance, a student took my hand, kissed it, and moved it to his forehead. Thinking that he was being disrespectful and possibly "showing me up," I jerked my hand away and forcibly put him back in line with the other students. Later I learned that he was not being disrespectful and, in fact, was showing me his regard.

We were told that, in international teaching, these anxious concerns can manifest themselves to produce behavior such as a loss or increase of appetite, intestinal problems, poor sleeping habits, irritability, and insecurity. A person's response to these problems is often referred to as culture shock. We all respond differently. In my case, I experienced excessive giddiness, the inability to concentrate, denial and detachment from reality, and the desire to participate in absolutely everything. I thought that culture change was the greatest thing that had ever happened to me. But as a family, we coped with change and culture shock in different ways.

I would describe Jennifer as a fiercely independent, bright

student who was disciplined and determined, though as vulnerable as any other sixteen-year-old girl would be. She had sought the adventure in Turkey, as she believed the experience would create and heighten the individuality she craved. As for Jean, although she did not go to Turkey against her wishes, this experience was not one of her long-range goals. She agreed that going to Turkey would be a one-time adventure and an opportunity to do something unique. She felt that this was her chance to step up and "go for it." As for me, you already know, I was searching for meaning in my life. Turkey happened to fit my exceedingly broad definition for what I thought would be a worthwhile experience. Mostly, however, I had conjured up a belief that my life would be unfulfilled if I never experienced living in a foreign country. It is obvious that we all had different needs and expectations.

Family arguments became more frequent several months after arriving in Turkey, and we found ourselves snapping defensively at innocent comments directed our way. The troubling signs were clear. Counseling was not an option or even deemed necessary, but it became evident that we had issues that needed to be addressed. I had believed that the overseas experience would be so uplifting that we would be immune to the stresses that typically affect people in our situation. Either my attitude led me to believe everything was fine, or I began internally blaming Jean or Jennifer when an issue evolved. I often thought that they were not mentally tough enough or lacked the ability or will to adapt. An accumulation of issues gradually wore us down and left us feeling unhappy. Our family of three would eventually learn how to deal with the phenomenon called culture shock, but this was not without pain.

Since I was the one who had pushed hard for this adventure, I tended to take responsibility for everyone's happiness, and I wanted to make things work. As problems arose, I became the fixer and conciliator, deeming it my duty to put out all fires. This proved to be unhealthy for everyone. We were slipping and sliding through our days and not coping. We were hindered by the lack of support from family and friends, and life in Turkey was getting difficult. My ever-present pride prevented me from admitting that there were problems; if there were any, they surely did not include me.

Our coping problems were compounded as Jennifer struggled with the Turkish curriculum—science and math in particular. The burden of learning new material, while attempting to catch up to her classmates, was becoming more difficult. She also found it hard to be fully accepted among her Turkish peers, and so the struggles grew. These realizations took a toll on her confidence. Up to this point, she had been remarkable and we admired her adaptability. Yet now, living a vastly different lifestyle, she felt lonely and missed her old friends.

"Why are we here?" and "Jennifer will never get into college with failing grades from Turkey" were comments I now heard. My responses changed from accepting responsibility to becoming defensive, and I began to offer my own set of blame.

As we attempted to work on our problems, the other issues of life in Turkey couldn't be dismissed. The water service was sporadic, leaving us without water for approximately five hours a day. Lack of phone service was disappointing because we were not yet connected. Language difficulties persisted. Add some stomach and digestive problems, the stress of teaching outside our comfort zone, cultural differences, loneliness, and the fact that we were spending an inordinate amount of time with each other, our causes were plentiful and real. Culture shock was alive and well.

Some of the adaptation process had gone well thus far. Though we missed the daily newspaper, TV sports, family, and friends, I was adjusting. Having the time to read was a luxury; I had begun reading the One-Year Bible, one day at a time, as well as countless other books.

Over time, the three of us found that we often just needed to say, "I need to talk," or "I'm not doing well today," or "How are you doing?" I had been especially guilty of being in my own world and ignoring my feelings as well as those of others. It had been easier to pretend that everything was fine than to deal with it. I realized my naivety in thinking that I alone could put out all the family fires.

In the past, I had used mission statements as a proactive approach to achieving goals and improving situations. So, we assiduously developed a family mission statement to help move us in a healthy direction. We decided that our family should be a place where we could truly be ourselves, while practicing patience and tolerance mixed with a lot of love and truth—just normal, healthy stuff that had been taken for granted at home. Our strategies were simple: we would assume the best in each other, admit our mistakes, and take responsibility for how we were feeling. The mission statement asked questions about our individual role within the family and what we expected from each other. We used these answers to form our mission statement, which Jean typed for each of us. We read it daily. We continued to talk and came up with ideas to propel us to help each other more and blame each other less. This led us to what would become the high point of each day: a time to sit down with a cup of tea and check in with each other. It wasn't therapy, but the components were there. We talked about our feelings, we laughed, and we cried. We openly discussed any frustrations we were feeling (that part was hard for me). We shared our successes, which could be as simple as mailing a letter at the post office or taking the bus to Alsancak by ourselves for the first time. The growth in our personal development was dramatic, and we began offering support where before we had been quick to blame. We still had many bad days, but progress was apparent.

Upsides and Downsides

Turkish lifestyle and culture were becoming more natural to me; yet, at some point each day, I found myself thinking: "I can't believe I'm walking down a street in Turkey." There were also other occasions when I pondered, "Why am I walking down a street in Turkey?" and "What does this mean for me?" Becoming more introspective and thoughtful might have been either the result of living in a foreign land or a sign that, at my age, I was finally becoming mature. In Turkey, however, I was always aware of my foreignness. Yet I liked and was comfortable with being a foreigner. Jennifer, on the other hand, always hoped she could blend in and pass for a green-eyed Turk.

International teaching had its upside—no lawn to mow, no repairs to make, no house to clean. We embraced our first-time experience of having a cleaning lady. It was an unencumbered life without a car or TV, no licenses or insurance to pay, and no garbage-pick-up day. Well there was a pick-up day, but the inescapable street cats usually disposed of much of the refuse each night.

Speaking of cats, one of the early morning thrills of living in Turkey was walking out the door with our tidy little white plastic waste bag in hand and tossing it in the open container on the street near our apartment. More often than not, two or three scrawny cats came leaping out, screeching and shocking me senseless. Their little black noses and whiskers were an unwelcome early morning sight. Between the morning ruckus and the late night rendezvous of our feline friends, I was no cat lover. Dogs were common as well and seemed to run in packs. They, too, lived on the streets and forced us to take care where we placed our feet. That caution was helpful, as the sidewalks were notorious for their ability to "take people down."

One of the most problematic aspects of foreign living was my desire to compare circumstances and solutions, and decide when, or if, I should step in. I was forever asking myself, "What would we do if we were at home in this situation?" The problem with this approach was that what might be acceptable in Turkey was not acceptable in the United States and vice versa. For example, I wrestled with this cultural dilemma in school faculty meetings. When it seemed that their problems were exactly the same as ones I had encountered back home, the solution appeared simple. Yet because this was a different culture, I was expected to keep quiet, or I believed that to be the case. I struggled with the tendency to say, "This is how we did it in America." The problem may have been fixed with our solution, but their culture might have frowned on the approach. We walked a fine line as teachers, for we were hired to serve, teach, and help others learn. If there was a better way to do something, we also had the obligation to contribute. I believe the word quandary would fit here.

While interacting with Turkish teachers was culturally and linguistically challenging, trying to make myself understood outside the campus was downright daunting. One of my most frustrating and helpless moments came while calling for a taxicab. Everything went well with my prepared speech, but it quickly disintegrated when I was unable to respond to the dispatcher's questions. Finally, in desperation, I threw my written speech away and hung up, not knowing if I had successfully ordered a cab or not.

On the other hand, at night I might be burdened with the remnants of the past day, but I typically awoke with excitement … and maybe a bit of fear of the "unknown" that the new day would offer.

Oh, how the memories stayed with me. They are stacked up, accessible when needed, and out of the way when not. That must be a result of heightened senses. The unpredictability of foreign living controlled our lives, and we had to accept that notion or be in trouble. Being vulnerable all the time felt good, but it was wearing.

Eating Like a Turk

It had become my weekend ritual to walk to Göztepe, our city neighborhood, to buy my favorite breakfast item, *gevrek*. *Gevrek* is the Turkish equivalent of a bagel, though larger, thinner, and tastier. The gevrek shop was located one block from the sea on Mithatpaşa Road, which was the major street in our neighborhood.

The bakery was small—I would call it a working man's shop—and quite different from an American bakery. All the baking was done adjacent to the counter in full view of the customer; I could reach out and touch the men making the *gevrek* dough. The four men alternately kneaded the dough and cooked it in the boiling oil. Then the dough was stretched and patted down in a box filled with sesame seeds. Using a long spatula, they next placed the dough in commercial ovens to bake.

The workers, dressed in T-shirts and tweed-like dress pants, continuously sipped tea and smoked cigarettes. Not once did I see a cigarette ash drift into the dough. When one sensed that the ash had become too long, he flicked it to the floor, took a sip of tea, put the cigarette back in his mouth, and resumed the kneading of the dough. Not the most hygienic environment, but at least I could see it for what it was. I took delight in the entire procedure; I think that the *gevrek* men sensed my joy and added a little extra flair to their work. They probably thought their antics gave the tall foreigner something to share with the folks back home, but I bet they didn't think I would include them in a book.

On one particularly cool morning, eager customers waited in a line that extended outside the shop. When I finally worked my way to the counter, the man stoking the ovens nodded at me, indicating that he recognized me. He knew the precise moment to slide the toasted bread out of the oven into a trough-like pan. Each piece of dough was toasted to a perfect caramel brown, never burned, always crispy. I, like each customer, grabbed a large piece of white glazed paper where I placed the hot *gevrek*. I had already paid in advance, so I could simply carry my purchase to the lone female who wrapped the *gevrek*. With quickness and dexterity she tucked and folded the pastry into a neat little package, and I was on my way.

I longed for the day when I would have the skills to wrap my own *gevrek* as most Turks did. I wasn't ready, but I was watching and learning. I left the store and wove my way through the mass of people, all waiting for what I carried. I climbed the hill toward our apartment clutching the *gevrek* to my body for warmth. My hunger grew as I anticipated the Turkish-style breakfast awaiting me. Our breakfast consisted of sliced tomatoes, sliced cucumbers, goat cheese, black salty olives, hot tea, and a variety of condiments that we added to the *gevrek*. I liked mine with cheese, while Jean and Jennifer dipped theirs in honey. Eventually, I hoped to enjoy my *gevrek* without the extras and eat it like a Turk.

The Turkish people are immensely proud of their cuisine. Initially we were skeptical, then hopeful, and eventually became believers. My first real Turkish meal had been in Istanbul during orientation. Our guide had encouraged us to "go Turkish." So, I'd ordered *iskender*, a speciality that included meat (I had lamb) on *pide* bread. The meat was covered with tomato sauce and a scoop of couscous. There was also a bitter white sauce on the top that we learned was unsweetened yogurt. Turks like yogurt so much that they even enjoy a whipped, tart yogurt drink called *ayran*. In fact, the word "yogurt" is derived from the Turkish *yoğurt*, an ancient staple of the Turkish diet.

Döner, which is the Turkish equivalent of the Greek *gyro*, became my favorite meal. Before we started any meal, however, we had *meze*, or Turkish appetizers. *Meze* included cheese, pickled vegetables, cold potato salad, olives, and the favorite for most Turks, *dolma*, or stuffed grape leaves. Bread is also a Turkish staple at only twenty-five cents a loaf; it is so good when fresh that it never needs butter. The Turks don't mind that it comes unwrapped, but Jean did. She never took the closest loaf in the bread case, instead reaching toward the back to the ones not yet squeezed. Or so she thought.

My sensitive stomach could not take the bitterness of Turkish coffee, which doubles the strength of most full-bodied

American coffee. Taking a sip of coffee with the grounds floating freely on the surface may have had something to do with the potency. The favorite Turkish alcoholic beverage is *raki*, which is similar to the Greek *ouzo*. It's anise-based, served in a large glass, and is customarily mixed half and half with water. The liquid is clear until the water is added, then a cool thing happens: it assumes a murky appearance. An acquired taste—which I never acquired—is in order for this surprisingly fortified drink.

Fairyland and Turkish Baths

Early in our first year, we received an unexpected two-day vacation for Turkish Independence Day. Many surprises took place during our stay in Turkey; this was one of the pleasant ones, for we had four days off, including the weekend.

About twelve foreign teachers (including Kurt, who was still visiting) rented a van with a driver and headed for eastern Turkey and Cappadocia, a barren land that originated with the eruption of two volcanoes. Over the years, wind, rain, erosion, and people transformed the landscape into an open-air museum. Nature formed an entire valley of columns and land bumps that are dispersed across the prairies and look like upside-down ice cream cones. The fairyland aura goes on for miles. Cave cities had been carved out of the rocks to serve as hideouts from the enemies for people who had once lived there (many of them persecuted Christians). We were allowed to climb and crawl in and amongst the underground city and could see the church frescos—wall paintings—amid the multi-leveled and intricate floor plan. Cappadocia is a true wonder. Even the caves have an air-conditioning system, which utilized the numerous openings and shafts to funnel breeze into these ancient living areas.

At another cultural excursion, early in our first year, seven men from the foreign-teacher crew headed to downtown Izmir to take part in Turkish nightlife. We went to Basmane, the old section of Izmir, located away from the sea where tourists normally hung out. The narrow and dusty streets were lined with people, and the lights were dim. Many men were seated around, while others were flowing in and out of the numerous shops. The women were less idle and seemed to have a purpose. The concrete buildings were dark, due to years of pollution. We stopped at an old teahouse that featured water pipes (*nargile*). The tea was good, but the water pipe made me nauseous. Next on the schedule—same location—was the chance to experience a Turkish (*haman*) bath, which for many of us was our first. There were many levels of service—I chose to wash myself and forgo the massage. I placed my clothes in a cubicle, was given a towel, and then led off to the hot bath where I lay on a marble table fighting to stay awake; the tranquility and subdued conversation were relaxing. I finished with a hot shower. Getting dressed was like wrapping lettuce around a cooked noodle. I could barely stand, let alone put my legs into my pants.

Basmane is very different from Westernized downtown Izmir. Most women wore long dresses and headscarves, regardless of age, and this seemed to add a touch of innocence to each of them. The headscarf also removed any individuality, which may have been the point. The men were fairly stoic and foreboding, with dark eyes that hid all emotion and faces covered with the shadows of whisker stubble. All male Turks, even those freshly shaven, inexplicably possesses a few days' growth. The heads of the elderly men were often topped with fisherman-type caps. They wear dark clothes and sport jackets, somehow staying cool in the heat of summer.

We left Basmane, walked several blocks, and concluded the night at an up-scale hotel that offered buffet dining and a belly dancing performance. The combination of a long day and a hot bath made me so tired that I slept through a portion of the event. (Yes, you heard right, I slept through my first belly dance.) I was reminded several times that I missed a good show.

Russian Piano and Beatles' Songs

We decided early on that both financial and time concerns would be secondary to what we wanted to experience in Turkey. This is my way of explaining why we bought a new Russian piano; we had the money and Jennifer had the interest. The decision to buy was easier than the process, because the owner of the music store wanted to be paid in American dollars ($2,000) due to the Turkish lira's high inflation rate. He convinced us that when we left in two years, he would return to us what we had paid for the piano. There was no contract between us, but I had been told he was an honest man. I thought that I understood the rationale behind the transaction and decided to place my trust in the Turkish businessman. Two men—one of whom was close to my age, but strong—carried the piano up the stairs and, in quick fashion, we had music.

As an aside, it was my understanding that installment buying, as we did in America, was not part of Turkish culture. A Turkish teacher, for example, bought a new car and paid cash for it. No debt—how un-American! People did not have checking accounts in Turkey. They dealt in cash, and if the cash is in American dollars, even better.

A further aside was that at the end of our two-year stay, I called the store and told someone that we were returning the piano. One week later, I stopped in the music store to explain in person to the owner that, "We are going home." He readily understood and went into the back room and came out with my $2,000. Never have I had a circumstance in my life where more trust was displayed by two men and from different cultures. An additional significant fact was that we didn't even know each other.

Jennifer loved having her own piano in the apartment that first year and was quick to play her classical pieces and Beatles' tunes. There was only one small glitch. One afternoon while Jen was playing, an extremely loud bang came from the wall of the adjacent apartment. It made us all pause. This banging continued over the next few weeks, proving that they weren't hanging pictures every day. Weeks later a very large Turkish woman screamed at Jennifer from her adjoining balcony, complaining (we presumed) that the piano music was too loud. We decided that it would be best for everyone if we moved the piano to another wall.

Activism Turkish-Style

There was talk in the school dining room one day of a tax protest that would begin that night. The protest would consist of walking to your door or balcony at 9:01 sharp. Once situated, you would bang kitchen pans together —or whatever your choice of noise makers—while yelling and whistling loudly to attract attention. (We decided that our wall-banging next-door neighbor would be good at this!) We waited in wonder and, exactly at 9:01, the noise began. We quickly moved to our balcony to observe the commotion, then rushed to get our only two pans, so we too could protest. Jennifer assisted by flicking the balcony light on and off. What fun! This went on for five minutes each night with the protest lasting for one week throughout all of Turkey. I am not certain of its effectiveness but, without question, all the politicians heard about the complaints. As their action involved the entire country, I thought it had more personal meaning than the activist protest marches that occur in the United States. Even though we didn't pay taxes in Turkey, I felt Turkish as we made our small but noisy contribution.

Turkey Day in Turkey

One instance of culture shock was celebrating Thanksgiving in Turkey. The most shocking piece was that we were invited to a Thanksgiving meal that was as tasty as we could have found any place in the good old USA. Our host family prepared a delicious dinner of chicken, pumpkin pie, and all the trimmings. Belma proved her skill in the kitchen with this exceptional meal and, of course, the very thoughtful gesture of friendship to her American friends. She and her family's acceptance of us helped make our transition easier.

Our host family's apartment was very modern, upscale, and large, with three bedrooms and two baths. The living and dining room areas were furnished with formal, elegant pieces, and the ceilings were adorned with white molding. French doors separated the rooms, and a balcony overlooked a lovely wooded park. Belma's extended family owned and occupied the four-story building. They all moved out for a year to completely refurbish the building, and the result was a beautiful apartment/home in a vibrant part of the city. The building would be a classy place in any city, in any culture.

Most often we were aware that we were in a foreign land. There wasn't much that I saw or heard in Turkey that would make me think of America. For example, the Turks didn't Americanize their words to accommodate Westerners: airport was *havaalani* and market was *çarşi*. However, that particular Thanksgiving—the first festive holiday away from our native land—felt just like home. We sat at the table, ate an American-style home-cooked dinner, conversed in English, and were surrounded by Westernized furnishings. Though we were vulnerable, the evening helped ease any pain of loneliness and emptiness that can be a part of living abroad, especially during an American holiday. We profusely thanked our host family, but it was difficult to convey to them the true gratitude we felt. On Thanksgiving Eve, we returned to our apartment rejoicing in what that experience had brought us, not lamenting what we had missed.

Yet we had not one, but two Thanksgiving celebrations. The second took place at the school and included both the foreign teachers and the Turks. Being active members of the social committee, Jean and I helped plan the evening of food, music, dancing, wine, and conversation. The event was held in the gym, but that did not detract from the celebratory holiday atmosphere.

A side-event to the celebration, however, created a bit of a distraction. Two days earlier, a parade of turkeys was herded across the campus. Five workers drove a dozen or so unwilling gobblers off to their demise, creating a commotion of feathers and muffled noise outside the classroom window. I had to admit that I had a flashback to that scene as I bit into forkfuls of my meat that Thanksgiving Day. Eating turkey in Turkey is not a usual occurrence, but it made for a food-filled and memorable week.

The dinner party was fun with the Turkish music and, of course, the dancing. We didn't make the mistake of offending anyone by playing western rock music as we did on Turkish Night several months earlier. We stuck to Turkish songs that allowed me to stomp and stumble my way though several dances, provoking laughter from Turks and foreign faculty alike.

Why? Just Because

I had made an early and arbitrary conclusion that our life in Turkey was similar to that of living in a Third World country. I held this belief in spite of the fact that there were modern buildings, an over abundance of cars, a number of upscale clothing stores, Westernized dress, a democratic governing unit, and an English-speaking school. I'm not saying that Turkey is a Third World country, but it continues to have some of those characteristics.

I remembered once reading an article that clarified the difference between living in a First World "why" country to that of a Third World "because" country. If you are in the United States, for example, and your bus is late or the elevator doesn't work, you ask "Why?" or "What happened?" The United States is considered a "why" country because we expect things to work, and we expect answers when they don't. In Turkey, people go straight to "because," as such delays and inconveniences are common occurrences. You could ask why, but the answer is typically, "Because, just because."

One situation with my basketball team illustrates these cultural differences. We had just arrived at another school for a scheduled scrimmage, when the other coach met us outside the gym and said in Turkish, "No scrimmage today; my players went home."

My exact words were, "Why! What happened?"

I asked one of my players to ask the coach to explain. They talked for a few seconds and my player returned to say, "The scrimmage has been cancelled." No why, not even a because.

"Why didn't he say something when our secretary called him this morning for confirmation?"

At this point, two players chimed in to further question the coach; he responded, my players shrugged, and they reported back to me, "The scrimmage was cancelled." They didn't express any bad will or anger—they didn't even ask, "Why?" They knew the answer already—"Because."

I never knew why these things happened; I only knew that they did, and it was part of the adjustment one made in this culture.

I did realize that my summation might be premature, as I had lived in Turkey only a few short months. My opinion, however, was based on how the culture functioned, what was accepted, and what life expectations were in general. All I knew was that the Turkish people had a high tolerance for "goof ups."

A Country in Change

My reflections are the result of the transformation going on in Turkey. There is a deep contrast between life in the country versus life in the city. Life can be difficult and ripe with poverty for many of those who have made a recent move from the country to the city. Those from the country tend to be more conservative in their beliefs and less educated; the women in particular are more apt to dress in *hijab* (a headscarf) and *tesettür* (a headscarf and light cover-all topcoat) than in Western-style clothing. There is also a continuous Turkish-Kurdish divide, most vehemently expressed in the cultural division between their language and traditions. Some Kurds have integrated into Turkish society, but most live in the east and hope for the establishment of their own country.

Izmir possesses neighborhoods that reflect not only various economic levels, but European versus traditional Turkish lifestyles as well. I mentioned Basmane as a section of Izmir that is traditional in dress and thought. In Göztepe, where we lived, the mixture of dress is indicative of the diversity in Izmir. Alsancak, the busy city center of Izmir, is European in look and clientele. If you were to take a bus from Göztepe to Alsancak and stop at the hub for a bus transfer, you would see Turkey for the divergence that it now offers. It would be common to see a young woman going to work in Alsancak in a short and fashionable skirt with high heels, while standing next to a woman covered in a full-length dress coat and *hijab*.

I made honest attempts to accept and appreciate what the culture offered. I had decided, and not without some difficulty, that though I was here to affect change, this influence should come from my teaching only. I did not want it coming from some philosophical discussion at a faculty meeting or a frustrated rant about the Turkish Ministry with friends. I was here as a guest of the country to teach and to experience a new culture. I had great hopes for the country and their wonderful people. They seemed to withhold their judgment of the foreigners and accepted us as we were. And we could be difficult at times.

It was important that we didn't take advantage of their good nature and somewhat compliant posture. We came here ignorant of the country and maybe a bit fearful; but from the first moment, I felt accepted and safe.

Christmas in a Muslim Country

Celebrating Christmas in a Muslim country was, of course, a different experience. Even though it was a normal school day, the Turkish staff, in a supreme act of goodwill, supported us by teaching our classes on Christmas Day. To further highlight the season, the city was decorated with wreaths and lights. The stores often displayed a small Christmas tree trimmed with care while Christmas carols could be heard in major stores.

It was our pleasure to attend a reverent and nostalgic Christmas concert at the U.S. Military Chapel. It was even possible to imagine that we were at a service in the United States, listening to children sing carols and read the Scriptures. This was all possible due to the small military base in Izmir and the many American families who lived there. It was an inspiring and thoughtful evening. Singing Christmas carols brought like-minded people together throughout the community and eased our loneliness and separation.

One experience that occurred shortly before Christmas was our purchase of a big cluster of holly branches—just like home, we thought. I cannot tell you how overjoyed Jean was when she spotted the branches, loaded with red berries. Now we would be able to decorate our apartment with an added holiday touch. Once home, we placed the branches in a large vase container and stood back to admire. Not until our foreign friends told us to look closely did we notice that each and every berry had been sewn on the branches to imitate the actual plant. Nevertheless, we enjoyed the color and festive appearance until well after the holiday season.

On Christmas Eve, we joined three families to dine at the Hilton Hotel. Our table, in a quiet room on the 31st floor, provided an impressive look at the brightly lit city. The car lights from the traffic moving alongside the distant harbor gave us our own candlelight service. It was beautiful and rendered a touch of sacredness to our secular setting.

Following dinner, we walked to church for a communion service and returned home by midnight. Our family was one of a few hundred people in this city of millions that worshipped and celebrated Christmas. God was with us and we with Him as we celebrated Jesus' birth.

We gave gifts for *Mütlü Yillar* (Happy New Year) to our Turkish friends. New Year's is a special event for them and this meant that gifts were in order.

During our first holiday season in Turkey, our foreign status felt especially acute. Back in the United States, whenever I saw foreigners, I used to feel some sympathy or maybe compassion. The fact that they were alone or separate from their family and their roots must have weighed heavily at times. We too felt our foreignness every day in Turkey—but I thought that this was a good thing. I didn't mind hopping on a bus and looking down the long aisle and seeing no one like me or making people wait as I struggled to make correct change on a bus or in a restaurant. It was part of the experience.

It was Jean with her dark hair, however, who often passed for a Turk. This posed a problem when, on the street or in a taxi, someone would talk to her in Turkish, expecting a reply. Instead, they got a blank stare from Jean and an apologetic answer in Turkish from the tall, slightly Nordic-looking teenager standing next to her.

New Year's Eve on Mineral Mountain

A very last-minute decision was made to visit Pamukkale and the wonderment the mountain offered with its thermal baths and crystal formations covering its entire side. The Pamukkale baths were rumored to have taken a beating over time from both tourists and pollution. The stress of walking amongst the baths had turned the once alabaster-like hillsides into a cinnamon color as the minerals in places had become polluted and darkened. We still wanted to go.

Jean, Jennifer, and I hopped on two buses and a *dolmuş*—mini bus—for the three-hour ride to Pamukkale. We had no plans or reservations other than a few general directions I had gathered in advance. Because we didn't have reservations, my mind was occupied with thoughts of getting a room over the busy New Year's holiday. This particular weekend ranked high on the list of important Turkish celebrations.

As we bounced along the road, I listened to two passengers talk to one another in Turkish. I understood only about one in every ten (make that twenty) words. I gathered that one of the men represented a *pension*, which was a small, reasonable hotel that offered limited services. He made his sales pitch to the other, and I was prepared for, but dreading, what would come next when he turned his attention to me. I was being "hustled," and it didn't feel good. He was aboard the *dolmuş* for one reason and that was to entice customers to his *pension*. Trying to ignore him, I pretended to have no idea what he was talking about, which I found came rather easily.

In due time the *dolmuş* stopped, we stepped off, and in my haste to get away from the hustler, I made a quick hand off and dropped Jean's camera on the ground, lens first. Here we were standing alone—well, not quite, as the hustler was right beside us—with a camera in questionable condition, with darkness quickly descending, and in the center of what looked to me to be a humble, if not broken-down, village. Jean was upset with me for dropping the camera, and I was upset at myself that we were in this predicament. Why were we deposited in the middle of what appeared to be nowhere, and where were the sparkling thermal baths we had read about in our travel brochures?

At the time, I was more bothered by the hustler than worried about the camera, a notion I did not dare mention to Jean. We were the only fools to have gotten off in the village. When the hustler earnestly urged that we go to his *pension* to fix the camera, Jean, whose only thoughts were focused on her broken camera, immediately perked up and said it was a great idea. We walked slowly along the deserted street, part brick and part dirt. It was becoming cool as the evening approached.

Eventually, the hustler stopped and pointed to his hotel, Ali's Pension. As we walked up the stairway, I said to myself, "There is no way Jean and Jennifer will stay here for a night."

Two questions needed to be answered. First, "How am I going to get us out of here?" And, second, "Where are we?" Pamukkale was supposed to be a major attraction and a huge tourist area, but this place was deserted and spooky.

We plopped our luggage down at a table in a dimly lit, stone-cold room. Jean immediately began working on her camera and on me.

I recall words such as, "Why did we come here?" and "How are you going to get us out of this place?"

Oh yes, Jennifer chimed in with, "I'm not staying here, for sure."

I ordered tea and a basket of bread and pretended to be interested in fixing the camera. Slowly I turned the telephoto lens cap that had been jarred off its tracks. The sound of grinding glass left everyone anticipating the worst. When the cap finally let loose, I cleaned the broken shards of glass away with my cold, numb fingers. Much to Jean's delight, only the glass in the protective lens had shattered, not the telephoto lens. Immediately, the tension in the room gave way to hesitant smiles. Jean grabbed the camera from me before I could do more damage. She was also quick to inform me that from now on I would not be allowed near her picture-taking machine.

I drank my last swallow of tea, felt amply fortified, declared that I had taken enough abuse from Jean, and informed the hustler that, "We are not staying in your *pension*." I had no ideas or plans beyond that decision. He was visually upset and tried to intimidate us into staying. In Turkish it sounded as though he said, "You'll be sorry." As we walked away, he continued to plead by telling us there were no other rooms available in this tiny village and that his was the best and cheapest the town had to offer.

Ignoring his pleas, I hoped that the rumors of a Turkish Mafia were not true. To add to our dilemma, it was now nearly dark. We hoisted our bags (Jean clutching her camera with both hands) and marched out into the cold, damp night. We didn't know at this point where we were or where we would stay, but we did know that it wouldn't be at Ali's Pension. Hopefully, we would find another inn to lay our heads.

We could see a sprinkling of bright lights in the distance at the top of what we thought was Pamukkale Mountain. We had no idea how we were going to get there and, more importantly, what was up there. Were the thermal baths at the top of the mountain?

Asking directions proved of little help and our confusion reigned. We finally garnered some vague information and began our trek up the side of a mountain. It would make sense that there must be a road somewhere. Up we went, eating some licorice I bought for sustenance.

Trekking up a path on wet, slick terrain covered with mineral deposits is more than tricky. We climbed, stopped to rest, were unsure of the way, but did know that the top of the mountain was our final destination. After thirty minutes, I judged that we were about half way up. Jennifer and I were carrying our luggage and backpacks; Jean had the camera, her fingers turning white with the tension in her grip and the cold of the evening. By this time we were walking in shallow pools of warm water that were trickling slowly downward as we moved upward. The air around us seemed to be getting warmer. All of a sudden, a shadowy figure walked toward us. Now what? As he came closer, he was whistling a tune, his hands in his pockets, as one would on a causal stroll. He didn't look stressed, but we sure were.

What a contradiction! I thought we were on a semi-life-threatening climb up a dangerously wet mountain, unsure if we would make it to the top. Would we slip and slide over the cliff's edge? Would the camera have to be thrown aside as the load got heavier and we became weaker? Would Jean throw me over the side to save her camera if the choice presented itself? All of these questions were displaced as we passed the casual Turk on an evening's stroll. We were safe and obviously not the adventurers we had imagined.

And then, the gift! At the top of the mountain were hotels galore. Our path had been a back route that brought us to the poolside of a large hotel. Our adventure was over and the camera would be safe for the night. The air was warm, the nervous tension had evaporated; in moments we would be relaxed, smiling, and who knows, maybe even ready for some serious picture-taking.

I woke up in a bright, cheery hotel room to early morning sunshine. Quick steps took me to the edge of our patio and a sight to behold. Snow-capped mountains stood in the distance separated by miles of valleys below. The lowlands were alive with the growth of the winter crop. Tractors were busy in the field, appearing like toys from my perspective. I hurried to wake up my traveling partners. We had gone to bed with a somewhat forlorn and negative perspective of Pamukkale, but with one quick glance at our daylight surroundings, our attitudes changed. We would stay longer than planned. We would wade in the warm baths. The daytime temperature of sixty-five degrees seemed much warmer. Life was good.

As a secondary gift, the ruins of ancient Hierapolis— churches, an amphitheater, columns, and fortresses—were scattered among the green countryside. We climbed the ruins and talked about what it must have been like those 2,000 years past. What had been accomplished long before was a marvel of design, discipline, and dedication. It was impossible to believe that these creations were achieved without the machines and technology that we take for granted today.

We celebrated New Year's Eve in an unusual way. I registered during the day for what I thought was a dinner and dance in the hotel's ballroom. After enjoying the day, we rested, dressed up, and at the appropriate time entered the main dining area.

We presented our name and were disappointed to find that we were not on the list. Ultimately, our name was found on another list, and we were ushered into a separate, colorfully decorated room with balloons and streamers. Very festive, I thought. We were seated and waited to be joined by others.

When the door finally opened, in rushed kids, lots of kids, all dressed in their finest. They were to be our companions for the New Year festivities. The parents seated the kids and then left to join the adult's celebration in the main ballroom. We were now catching on to the fact that we would be celebrating and bringing in the New Year with sixty kids who looked to be between the ages of five and fifteen. The parents returned frequently to check on their children, who were well behaved. The same could be said for us. Just before midnight, we bravely sauntered over to the ballroom to listen to the band play and to watch the adults from the entryway with the "other" children. I felt like an intruder or, at least, an unwanted observer. Eventually, I gathered up my sense of worth and asked both Jean and Jennifer to dance. We joined in with the revelers for a Happy New Year! I couldn't speak Turkish, but I could dance Turkish.

ONLY IN TURKEY!

I am certain that spending time in any new culture provides an assortment of moments or events that leave a person to question, "Did that really happen?" Who are these people called Turks? What are they like, how do they think, and why do they do things a certain way? This section will recall those occasions, some of which were dramatic, some funny, and quite a few that were capable of making me shake my head in wonderment, smile to myself, and say, "Only in Turkey."

Time for a Change

Change is typically a difficult process to undergo for individuals and, equally, for groups, organizations, or countries. Do you recall when the United States tried to change to the metric system? It could not be done. Well, our friends the Turks woke up one morning to learn that a major cultural component, their language, would be changed in three months time. And by the way, they would also be forbidden to wear the fez (a distinctive red Turkish cap) that was a traditional part of their culture.

This would be a significant policy change to undergo for a young democratic nation like Turkey, but such an occurrence took place in 1928. For reasons of literacy and in the interests of progress, President Atatürk decided to replace the Arabic alphabet with the Latin alphabet. He pushed this task through quickly; in a matter of weeks it was forbidden to speak in old Arabic. During a subsequent speech, Atatürk threw his fez away, placed a Western-styled fedora on his head, and said, "No more fez." And so it was in the fledgling Republic State of Turkey.

The new Latin alphabet had a few oddities for the Turks, but it also had the benefit of being a phonetic language. I had my own inadequacies with the Turkish language, but I appreciated the concept of having one sound for each letter of the alphabet. For example:

A, a	short "a" as in "art" or "bar"
E, e	"eh" sounds like our long "a"
O, o	same sound as in English
Ö, ő	put your lips into a small "o" shape and try your best—this one is hard
C, c	pronounced like our "j" as in "juice"
Ç, ç	"ch" as in "church"
G, g	hard "g" sound like "get"
ğ	silent, not pronounced—Türkoğlu, pronounced TUR-ko-lou
J, j	pronounced like our "zh" as in "azure"
S, s	always "sss" as in stress, not "zzz" as in "ease"
Ş, ş	"sh" as in "show"
W, w	exists only in foreign words; not really Turkish

The main advantage of the Turks' new language was that there were no double-letter sounds, so the letter was pronounced as you saw it.

"Can" is pronounced	John
"Evet" (yes) is pronounced	eh-VEHT
"Pardon" is pronounced	parh-DOHN
"Çok" (very) is pronounced	choke
"Doktoroğlu" is pronounced	doctor-o-lou

The pronunciation was fairly easy for me, but the grammar and word order were difficult. In Turkish, verbs and subjects are placed at the end of the sentence. In English, we would say, "I'm going to school," while Turks would arrange the sentence, "School to going I am" ("*Okule gidiyorum*"). The task of learning a new language is confusing for an already confused mind, but I relished the effort to learn and took pride in what Turkish I could speak.

Our "Friend," the Water Depot

We were subjected to many inconveniences that became more than an annoyance as the year progressed. Due to a perpetual water shortage in the city, the water was turned off in some apartments—including ours—every day from noon until 5:00 p.m. The problem became particularly bothersome on weekends and holidays when we were often home. To our relief, the administration deemed this an unsatisfactory arrangement for a foreign family. The typical solution to resolve the water shut-off problem in Turkey was to install a water depot on the roof of one's building as a mechanism to store water. Instead, we became the recipients of a giant, two hundred-gallon tank, which resided in our spare bathroom.

The concept behind the water depot was that we would never be without water. During those times when the city would shut off the water, we would then call on our friend the water depot. That sounded good and proper, and we were appreciative of the school's effort to accommodate our needs. But there were issues.

Let me tell you about our new friend, the water depot. I know that this will sound ungrateful, but the thing was immense and an intrusion in our home—it was placed in a horizontal position, completely commandeering the spare bathroom. It made mysterious-sounding noises, like at 3:00 a.m. when it creaked and shook the apartment. There was a perspiration problem as well. It was my contention that it merely wanted to be outside with the other water depots. That makes sense, doesn't it? Yet it should be noted that it did nothing to conserve water.

One morning the depot was to be filled while we were at school. The automatic shut-off valve was programmed to kick in when the depot was full, and we would then have access to water. I came home from school early, and as I walked up the stairs was puzzled to see a steady flow of water cascading down. Uh-oh, I thought, someone's sink is overflowing. My worst fears were confirmed when I saw that the water was coming from our apartment. Four inches of water covered our entire floor. The water depot had kept me awake at night, and now it had let me down during the day. It remains too painful and unnecessary to go into the details of the clean up, but the reason as to why most water depots are placed outside on the roof of a building had become clear. Only in Turkey!

Haircut—A Gala Affair

At home in Minnesota, going to the barber was one of my least favorite things to do. Unlike going to the dentist, haircuts were not painful, but I avoided them as long as possible. When I did get a haircut—without Novocaine—I would typically walk around with a look that said, "Look who just got a new haircut." I was not one of those guys who looked the same when he came out as when he walked into the barbershop. I am providing this

PHOTOGRAPHS

ACI Administration Building

Year One Apartment Building

The Three Foreign Students at the Opening Ceremony

Family Tour of Ephesus

PHOTOGRAPHS

Library at Ephesus

Cappadocia Landscape

Year One Basketball Team

Atatürk Day at ACI

PHOTOGRAPHS

Pamukkale Thermal Baths

Pamukkale Hierapolis Ruins

Camel Wrestling

Orta Guidance/Physical Education Class

PHOTOGRAPHS

Turkish Village Children

Nepalese Shave

Circumcision Celebration

The Old Course at St. Andrew's

information to the reader for some background into why I was apprehensive to get my haircut in Turkey.

It was the result of good planning on my part that I was presentable (good old neck trims) even though twelve weeks had passed since my last haircut in the United States. I was not as particular about style as I was about length. How could I explain this to a barber? One veteran teacher told me about the "point-at-the-knuckle method," which involved the index finger. From the tip to the first knuckle indicated just a trim; second knuckle, a regular-type cut; and the third knuckle, heaven forbid, meant a major shortening. Sounded good to me, and I decided to use the knuckle method as a backup plan.

Family pressure had pushed me to walk into the small barbershop down the street from our home. The invariable and timely admonition, "Don't get it cut too short this time," was rattling around in my head. In fact, that warning was still there from my last haircut, and every one I'd had in the previous thirty years.

I had walked by this shop many times, but this time was for real. Nervous, I walked in. The shop held two barber chairs and one barber. I evaluated his hair at first glance and liked what I saw. His close-cut, light brown hair hugged his head. This guy didn't even appear to be Turkish. He had a swagger to his walk and a confident hand. I calculated that this man with the scissors knew what he was doing. One customer sat in the chair and a second one was waiting. A small TV was playing, but no was watching. I smiled, said "*Merhaba*," and sat down.

I wanted to watch, and the barber wanted to perform. The scissors acted like a part of his hand when they moved through the man's hair. Instead of trimming the sideburns with a safety razor, the showman whipped out his straight-edged razor and whapped it against the leather strap for effect. He slapped on some shaving cream and scraped it away with a single swipe of his weapon. Then the grand finale! He grabbed from a cabinet shelf a device that would make a welder proud. With a flourish, he lit it and singed the sideburns of the man in the chair.

The barber stopped and looked at me as if to say, "When was the last time you saw anything like that in an American barbershop?"

Never have and never will, I was thinking. My grin accompanied an affirmative nod of my head.

I smiled as I climbed into the chair, wishing I could express myself by telling him to gimme the works! I had already forgotten all about the knuckle method, and I was no longer afraid. I had trust. I gestured at his hair and with a scissors cutting hand motion I pointed at mine. He nodded knowingly and gave me an "aha" look as he walked toward a shelf that held an old fashioned tape player. He turned off the TV and shuffled some old tapes around until everything was finally in order. He pushed a button and stepped back as an Elvis tune, "It'll Be a Blue Christmas Without You," wafted through the small room. He swaggered toward me, his body moving in rhythm to the song and his head nodding to the beat of the music. What we were having was one of those special moments that could only take place between a barber and the man in the chair. While Elvis sang, the scissors danced and flicked, and when the blowtorch made its appearance, I didn't flinch an inch. The bill was $2.80. I gave him a $5.00 tip and walked out of that shop and down the street with my head high, a strut in my step, and a renewed presence.

"You look like a kid," someone said later.

In place of my old bemused smirk, I now had a cocky grin and quipped, "Short hair will do that, you know."

Splat!

One day Jean and I exited the bazaar area and walked the narrow streets of Izmir. I was slightly ahead of her as we worked our way through the maze of people and an ongoing construction site. Suddenly I heard Jean shriek with the urgency appropriate in an ambush attempt: "I've been hit! I'm hit!" Turning quickly, I saw Jean's face sullied with a huge splat of gray matter. Remnants of wet cement hung on the scaffolding directly above. I pulled her off to the side, got out the ever-ready Kleenex pack, and, between a few muffled giggles, tried to clean her up.

What she needed was a good trowel. Wet cement stuck in her hair, on her clothes, and yes, in her clothes. I did the best I could with what I had to work with on the busy streets of Izmir. Jean finished the clean-up job in the bathroom of the nearby Hilton Hotel by dipping her shirt and her head under the faucet. When she exited the bathroom her face was shiny clean, her clothes had that cement stain look that will never catch on, but her hair was slicked back with a smooth mortar appearance that may become popular.

Too bad that the "hit" wasn't a big bird dropping on her head, as that is a sign of good luck in Turkey. We don't know what getting pummeled with wet cement means, so we'll have to wait and see what the future brings. Only in Turkey.

Trips, Falls, and the "Runaway Man"

Numerous falling stories abound in Turkey. One day during the first few weeks of school, a principal arrived with a black eye, broken glasses, and numerous cuts and abrasions around her nose and chin. We thought the worst about her situation until we learned of the fickleness of the steps and sidewalks of Turkey.

It was a rainy day on campus, and I had taken brief refuge in the Administration Building. Out the window, I saw a familiar figure in a green trench coat hurrying down the checkerboard path of concrete squares. One moment Jean was upright and the next she was down. Her feet flew upward, launching her rain boots into space. This proved to be a good thing as one of those same boots provided a resting-place for her head, which ended up under the plethora of bushes. Before my body responded to action, I must admit to some amusement. Someone standing next to me exclaimed, "Isn't that your wife?" I recovered quickly, stifled my laughter, and ran out to the victim. "Are you alright?" Other than her scuffed knees and hands, the answer was yes. Except, of course, for the embarrassment and hope that no one had noticed—especially her students. As I lifted her up from the soggy ground, she removed the shrub branches protruding from her hair, rescued her boots, and was on her way.

One of my more memorable falls on campus came at the end of a thirty-some-step climb. This was a climb that I, and most others, avoided when possible. I was nearing the top with my briefcase slung over my right shoulder while balancing three books in my left hand. The concrete of the top step—with knowledge from previous trips—was a bit thicker and more uneven than the other steps. Danger was always lurking, and I lost my concentration. As I placed my foot down on the last uneven step, my rubber-soled shoe "grabbed" and my knee buckled. My body began lilting to the right, and, eventually, the lilt turned into a freefall. My body was in a slow-motion pattern that allowed me to think of a plan of action. Realizing there were bushes to the right of the steps, and I had a stuffed briefcase to cushion my blow, I let my body fall to the ground. It was a good fall, maybe my best fall ever, as awarded by sixty years of ungainliness. To qualify as a good fall, there should be no detection, a minimum of embarrassment, and no permanent injury. A quick check of limb and inner being proved to be negative, and I was off and running, a bit better prepared to handle what the day ahead would bring.

Eye contact is not part of the Turkish culture, or at least when a person is in motion. Making eye contact while walking could be a disaster for even the most nimble and sure-footed. On one occasion, while walking in a newer area of Izmir, I caught my toe on a raised piece of concrete. Jennifer grabbed my shirttail from behind and kept me upright as I careened down the sidewalk as passersby cleared the way. The visual of a gangling foreigner falling, arms flailing, nose diving to the ground, and a young girl running behind hanging onto the back of his shirt, did little to enhance our American image. I learned a valuable lesson that day—no more eye contact.

Turkish Generosity

One day in December, we saw a Christmas pillow in a store window. Such an item seemed out of place in Turkey. Jean was delighted, since it reminded her of the approaching holiday. We inquired about the price. Surprisingly, the clerk said that it was not for sale. We assumed she misunderstood, but further questioning brought the same response. We continued to look around the store and, on preparing to leave, the clerk handed Jean a bag. Confused, we peered inside to see . . . the pillow. Again we asked how much. The clerk snapped her head upward in a quick motion that Turks use to signify "no." It finally became clear; she was offering it to us as a gift. We implored the clerk to let us pay, but again she refused. We left the store with the pillow feeling guilty and overwhelmed by her generosity.

(To better grasp the technique of saying *no* in Turkish, follow along with these directions, complying with both the movement and sound effects. Hopefully you are alone and not in a public place. Lift the chin upward with a slight snap, raise the eyebrows, and with the tongue on the roof of the mouth, make a tsk-tsk sound. This motion is used with a flourish in Turkey, and it became an endearing gesture for us. In fact, we found ourselves imitating this same motion long after returning home to America.)

One evening Jean and Jennifer leisurely dined at an outside restaurant near the water. Sitting at a small table covered with a white tablecloth and topped with a colorful umbrella, they ordered the usual—margarita pizza, salad, and cola. Later when the bill was presented, they searched both purses for Turkish lira and came up short. A slight panic set in as they tried to calculate what they should do. The bill came to 1.2 million Turkish lira, and their collective sum was 750,000 Turkish lira. Jennifer explained their predicament to the waiter—Jean didn't have the words!—telling him that they would quickly walk the three blocks home and return with the amount required. He smiled and replied with the expected, "No problem." Oh good, they thought. We won't be arrested and put in the notorious Turkish prison. Instead, the waiter reclaimed the bill, peered down at the small, faded slip of paper (think kitchen note pad) and then hastily changed the bill total to match the amount of lira they had. Nobody would be that creative in America. Only in Turkey!

Another reason to love the Turkish people—we returned later to pay the full amount and, naturally, the restaurant refused to accept it.

More "Because"

By January of our first year we still hadn't succeeded in getting a phone. My frustration had grown to such a level that I needed to express my exasperation to the foreign faculty coordinator. Six months to install a phone seemed a bit much, and I placed the responsibility directly on the school. I concluded that they should have permanent phones installed in each apartment and each subsequent dweller could rent the phone. The Turkish bureaucrats had also increased the installation fees, compounding the problem. On a bright note, our phone bill was zero because, in addition, the phone cards we had purchased didn't work.

When the telephone company finally arrived to provide the phone hookup, they discovered that our apartment was already equipped with a hook-up and needed only an actual phone to be service-ready. We had waited from September to February to receive service and it had been there all the time. I took the news well, and muttered to myself, "Only in Turkey."

The bank was another source of frustration. Because travel agencies often required American dollars and wanted to be paid in cash, I had the foresight to deposit a $6,000 check in my

Turkish bank in anticipation of a mid-year trip and the purchase of the aforementioned piano. I was told that it would take a month or so for my check to clear and for the bank to obtain that much in dollars. At the given time I would be able to withdraw the money in American dollars, all $6,000. I entered the bank to retrieve my cash. I was met with the inevitable surprise, in this instance a shortage of dollars.

There I stood at a wide counter with people on either side of me. There was no orderly line, no "stand back while the customer in front of you completes their transaction," and no partitions. The other customers hovered around the counter as if they were at the local meat market. If in need of assistance, I am certain that the person or persons standing next to you had gathered enough personal and financial history to conduct your business for you. On this particular occasion, I waited close to thirty minutes to speak with a bank employee with English-speaking skills. She explained that they did not have enough American dollars to pay me.

After forty-five minutes of frustration and discussion with four different people, I was not happy. I left the bank with about $4,000 American dollars and the balance in Turkish lira, which I didn't want or need. The money was counted three times and then heaped onto the small ledge of the counter. I was totally unnerved; I had trouble counting money in English, let alone Turkish. I found myself looking around to see who might be a prospective thief. My friends, the Turks, suddenly all fit that image, with their unshaven faces, their sinister-looking brown eyes, and their hands vanishing out of view. Did they have a weapon? My paranoia was in full bloom. I had planned on leaving with $6,000 American dollars in denominations of one hundred, all neatly folded in my pocket. Now I was walking out of the bank with $4,000 dollars in multiple denominations coupled with an armful of Turkish lira that was stuffed into every available pocket on my body.

Nervously, I left the bank and hurried down the street,

suspecting everyone and glancing behind to see how much I may have dropped. If I dropped anything, I hoped that it was Turkish lira. I made the three-block walk safely and without incident. After bounding up the stairs, I locked the door, leaned back against it as is done in the movies, and exhaled with relief.

Another frustrating circumstance occurred when several of our athletic teams scheduled a trip to our sister school one weekend. Extensive plans, which included housing, transportation, and fees, were in place and the students' anticipation was high. We were to take one hundred students to Tarsus, Turkey, a trip of several hours, to play in a well-planned sports festival. Unexpectedly, the Turkish vice principal called me out of an afternoon meeting with the news that the trip might be cancelled.

In a calm voice she told me, "The Turkish Ministry has changed the rule regarding insurance requirements for student travel. Each student must have individual insurance coverage, and we have one hour to comply." The policy change apparently came as a result of several school bus accidents in the country, and the fact that one of our own students had been killed the previous fall while riding to school.

I was shocked. "Do we have the time to honor that request?"

"No. We'll have to cancel the trip."

Prior to this news, a blanket insurance policy covered all school trips. Now, an individual policy was required to match each name on the bus passenger list. There was no chance that we could comply in the one-hour window. All the students were hastily called that night; the disappointment was universal. I was amazed, however, at the acceptance and understanding from the students. They were seriously disappointed, but they exhibited an attitude of "that's the way things always go here." More than one student said, "I knew something would happen. I knew we wouldn't go."

As for me, I was crushed. I took the cancellation personally. As the administrator in charge, I was responsible and believed I had let them down.

IT'S A BALL!

Playing and coaching basketball has been a major part of my life. Many of my happiest, most serene and reflective childhood moments were spent playing the game. Yet, it was not playing the actual game as much as shooting by myself in my driveway that created the passion that spurred me through my adult life. My clearest and most satisfying basketball memories are of those as a small boy—in the heart of a cold winter, putting up shot after shot on the driveway of my home in small-town Minnesota. Neither the basket rim that was askew nor the uneven, snow-packed ground was an obstacle for the heavily booted shooter. Nor did the gently falling snow or the well-worn chopper mitts deter me.

I was a lone figure on that driveway, but surely not lonely. I was inspired to play. I had found my peace. I grew to love the solitude of those moments, moments of course that would prepare me for the ultimate, which was playing the game. My goal was not to be a prize athlete, just to do what felt good and seemed right—and that was play ball. Basketball eventually determined where I would go to college, what I would do with my life, and where I would do it. I would become a coach, I came to love the profession, and now it had brought me around the world.

It was my decision to coach while we lived in Turkey. After thirty-five years as a head coach, I would have been uncomfortable and restless teaching and not coaching. During my teaching career, I had two opportunities to "get away," and did so only because it allowed me to coach. The year Jean and I were married, I left a good job to work on and complete my master's degree at the University of Minnesota. I immediately inquired about coaching possibilities; the result was a year spent helping with the freshman basketball team. After twelve years of teaching at Wayzata, I received a sabbatical leave to attend and coach at the University of Virginia. I helped with an outstanding national caliber basketball team, while studying adaptive physical education. In other words, my history included the positive impact that coaching made on my life during these two transitional periods. It was my hope that coaching might offer a deeper and more unique look into the Turkish culture. I would not be disappointed.

Play Ball!

Our team had just finished our third basketball practice. We practiced in a gym right out of the 1940s: six baskets with rims at various angles to the floor. The floor, about two-thirds the size of a regulation-sized floor, was uneven, had numerous dead spots, and produced more bad bounces than a Chicago road. You could make a case for it being dangerous, but if you fell through, the fall would not be far.

We began our basketball practices in September. We had limited gymnasium facilities, but we did have access to three outside courts. To say that the program and philosophy of sports was different in Turkey is an understatement. The season ran all year, regardless of when the games were scheduled, and that presented distinct problems in scheduling our facilities. I never knew when my schedule of games was to begin, but scrimmages were at my disposal. I had been warned to be prepared at all times. It sounded crazy.

The team had a number of good athletes who were mostly Lise 3 (senior) students. They were lacking in basketball fundamentals, but appeared to be coachable. If I could teach them to play with more discipline and improve their fundamentals, we might be able to play with the average teams. Our biggest problem was the lack of practice time together, since seniors could practice only on Fridays. So during the remaining week-days, I made an effort to coach them at their separate lunch breaks, working on individual skills.

The life of a Turkish student-athlete differed from the life of an American student-athlete in regards to balance and perspective. At ACI, academics came first in all regards. Finding a balance was the goal in my previous coaching positions, but sports would often supercede. There were also schools in Turkey where athletics were emphasized, but those students, in all likelihood, would be unprepared to pass the difficult university exams.

The student-athletes at ACI truly did not have a choice. Due to the competitiveness of the university exams, their youthful lives were completely dominated by their academic goal of getting into the right university. Extra-curricular activities were just that—extra—and only if the time and energy were available. And, for most it wasn't. Maybe our two cultures could learn something from each other.

Three of my players invited me to attend a professional basketball game, an unconventional and entertaining event. The fans were intensely involved and showed their enthusiasm with cheers and jeers. The arena, in the heart of Alsancak, was dirty and dingy even though the building was not old. The fans, however, made the dreary arena come alive with their energy and their Turkishness; they chanted, whistled, and, yes, even threw coins on the floor.

It's Practice Time

The moon, which peered through the towering campus trees, and the shaded light of a weary lamppost provided just enough illumination to allow practice to continue beyond sunset. Shadowy figures could be seen cutting to the basket, but the grunts of effort and the squeaks of shoes were better heard than seen. The mission of this practice was to concentrate on patience, to hold the ball for two counts, and to be aware of the floor (and other players) at all times. For me, outside practice tended to take away the intensity of the game. The kids, however, responded well; this might have suggested the familiarity of the site for them, and that was what counted. This was basketball in Turkey.

The Playoffs

By November, the time had come to play in the Turkish Ministry-controlled playoffs. We had practiced four times with all the players present, coupled with individual workouts. We were in a bracket with two other teams, and we would all play each other. The team with the best record would move on and the other two teams would be out, finished for the season. We played a team that was supposedly not as good as we were. That proved to be true, and we won handily. The boys played hard and, considering our lack of practices with the entire team, they performed well.

The next day we faced the dreaded Maltepe, a military school with a highly trained and efficient team. Our season basically ended. Yes, I know that the season had only started the day before, but that was the system. Maltepe downed the under-manned—I didn't say poorly coached—ACI boys, but we hung in there for a half. Our 2–3 zone worked well at keeping the score close, while we played conservatively and at a slow strategic pace.

It was determined that if we had a next game, it would be at our sister school in Tarsus, about four months later. That team would consist of the younger players, as the seniors would have dropped out to continue studying for the university exams. The system was bizarre, but there was no way I could change it. It seemed to me that a reasonable solution would be to create a conference with the nearby schools and play a regular schedule of games before the Ministry playoffs began. That would offer incentives to practice and improve, plus give the players the excitement and motivation that comes with playing games.

Random Sports Event

Quite by chance, on my way home from Alsancak one Saturday afternoon, I came upon the local arena. Karşiyaki, a team from Izmir, was playing Beşiktaş, a team from Istanbul. I had no commitments—no windows to wash, lawn to mow, or leaves to rake. I bought a ticket. I was both surprised and impressed with the high caliber of the players. The level of play could compare to a U.S. Division I college program. Each team happened to have two American players who did not dominate play; the remaining players were Turks. Just the presence of the American players made me feel less lonesome.

The game was well played and exciting as Karşiyaka won in the last second. My favorite cheer was a local chant: "Kof! Kof! Kof! C! C! C! Kof-C, Kof-C, Kof!" About fifty police escorted the fans down the street as the celebration moved out of the arena in typical Turkish fashion (banners flying, cars honking, people cheering). I moved with the crowd. It was all in good fun. I decided to celebrate in my own way with a Western meal at a new restaurant called the British Pub.

One day, I watched a special awards ceremony from a bench next to the Administration Office. It was a formal dress-up day, and everyone looked sharp in their navy blazers. What struck me was the genuineness of the students as they cheered and clapped for the award winners. They appeared to be magnanimous and totally selfless in their response. I was very proud of my basketball players for they dominated the male component of the ceremony. They were not basketball stars, but they possessed the attributes that really mattered to be successful. Although I played no part in their accomplishments, I was proud to know them and happy to see that their achievements matched my view and opinion of them. The entire ceremony reflected how close the students had become during their school career. There was no sophistication or phony pride about being chosen for an award. Everyone felt that it was a big deal. To further demonstrate this behavior, a player named Hassan was given a standing ovation for his seven years of perfect attendance.

TIMEOUT!
LET'S GO FAR... EAST

Timeouts in the sports' world were originally designed to produce a break in the action or a brief physical rest. Timeouts today have become a means for coaches to manage the game and manipulate the situation to their team's advantage—to set up plays, "freeze" a shooter, and so on. I will use our timeouts for the original purpose . . . to gather and compose oneself to enable the player to come back to the game with renewed vigor and purpose.

Saint Augustine said, "The world is a book, and those who do not travel, read only one page." It was our plan to be avid "readers" and devour as many pages as we could. We had never traveled abroad, so this would be our time. We would have ample opportunity for lengthy trips with a three-week semester break and two-month summer vacations. An abundance of long weekends gave us occasion to visit sites within Turkey. Travel proved to be one of the major benefits of foreign teaching, and the staff was in perpetual planning for their next trip. For me, travel proved that teaching abroad was truly a fantasy-like experience.

Istanbul

After the completion of our first school semester, we were off to Istanbul, but not on the Orient Express. We would stay in

Istanbul for two days before flying to Kathmandu, Bangkok, and Singapore. Going off to exotic Asia was more than a little daunting. We were going to Nepal to face everything that a Third World country had to offer. Our anxiety was lightened by the fact that Kurt would meet us at the airport in Kathmandu.

We arrived in Istanbul feeling good about having completed a semester of school. We were tired but energized for the trip. After checking into our hotel, I wandered down the street to seek out a new section of the town. When in doubt as to what to do, eating is always a good choice. While munching on a sandwich, I casually gazed through the big window overlooking the crowded street. My eyes wandered from the bus stop to the inter-section, which were both full of people. Unexpectedly, I felt that I was being watched and glanced up to see a typical-looking, short, dark-haired Turkish man observing me. Well dressed in casual clothes, he quickly waved at me as our eyes met. At first, I thought he was motioning to someone behind me. That was not the case, so I turned back to face him and although I felt a bit uncomfortable, I nodded back at him. While I stood on the curb waiting for the light to change on my way back to the hotel, I sensed someone standing beside me. It was him.

"You from America!" came the stock greeting. Or was it a question?

"*Evet*," (yes) I responded to let him know I knew Turkish. Feeling more uncomfortable now, I moved away and bid good-bye. The light changed and incredibly he was matching me stride for stride as I crossed the busy street.

"Do you want to buy leather?" "*Hayir*," (no) I answered.

"I have great carpets also," he quickly replied.

"*Hayir*," I said becoming more annoyed, partly at myself because I had gotten into this situation. I tried to explain to him that I lived in Turkey and was not a tourist. He then pulled out his billfold and showed me his ID card (why did he do that?). I inspected his card (why did I do that?).

As I walked down the street he shocked me with his next

question: "Do you want sex?"

"Sex?" I replied harshly and heard myself repeat the word all the while wondering how we made the leap from carpets to sex. My mind was unable to sort this out. What does he want? I wondered. What does he think I want? If someone says *no* to buying a carpet, is that code for wanting sex?

These futile questions took mere seconds before I yelled "No!" as I threw my arms in the air. I really wanted to punch him, but reminded myself that my last fistfight was thirty years earlier in a basketball game, and that didn't go well.

I pointed at my hotel a block away and yelled down at him, "I'm going to see my wife and daughter so leave me alone." He merely turned and walked away. I had never been propositioned before, and the experience left me shaken. I recovered from my trauma by drinking tea and sharing my story with Jean and Jennifer. It was a family decision that I not be allowed to wander by myself in the streets of Istanbul.

Nepal

As we approached Kathmandu, our anxiety level grew. We were eager to see Kurt but had a healthy skepticism about Nepal. The airport runway was tucked into the valley, and the sharp descent made for a dramatic landing.

The customs wait was endless. People milled all around me while I surveyed the scene. I was a giant amid the Nepalis. Seeing Kurt beyond the roped off area where we were waiting in line reassured me. He would ease our entry into the authentic Third World. It was a good feeling to be able to look to your children for support. But would we have a good time? Would we get sick?

Kurt had a small (tiny) taxi waiting. The four of us squeezed in and were off, weaving our path toward the city. My first look out the side window kept my attention. Could it be? . . . it was . . . a golf course! I had not seen one in Turkey, so I surely never expected to see one in Nepal. Literally, the course was a goat pasture with more goats than golfers, yet it would be the first of several examples of Western life in Nepal that was not available in Turkey.

Our driver took us through a maze of streets filled with people, chickens, small cars, cows, rickshaws, and hundreds of ruts that kept us alert. It was a stop and start kind of road—definitely not a thoroughfare.

We arrived at the Hotel Mountain and were surprised to find a very updated and pleasant establishment. The rooms were modern and clean; the hotel even provided dry cleaning services—nothing that we'd expected. After settling in, Jean decided to take a short walk to familiarize herself with her surroundings. I watched from the hotel window as she came face to face with a cow casually taking a stroll down the sidewalk. Jean moved aside to provide enough space for the sacred cow as it peacefully and confidently passed. There were more cows on the sidewalk than Americans, so that determined the right of way. We were adapting.

After a short rest, we walked down the street with Kurt to the *Phora Durbar* "the country club" where expats ate, relaxed, and played. As we unwound with a soft drink and sandwich, I began to experience some relief from my uptightness and appreciated the fact that we were safe in Kathmandu. The club consisted of several acres of grounds, walking paths, green grass, and basketball courts. It was a dramatic step away from the chaos in the streets, and it provided the Peace Corps and Embassy folks a quiet, though not fancy, retreat.

The Indian style meal at the Hotel Mountain that evening was delicious. Jean was more attracted to the salt and pepper shakers than the food on the table and embarrassed us by making repeated attempts to buy them. Our waiter was completely confused by her offer and just smiled and was on his way. I had a talk with her.

The next morning took us to Ringmos, a Peace Corps hangout, where we ate our first American breakfast in six months.

We were almost giddy as we ate the pancakes, French toast, and scrambled eggs. Even the toast was a delicacy to our deprived American pallets.

A tour through the Peace Corps offices showed us that we Americans were receiving a good return on our tax dollars. We met some very nice people who Kurt was acquainted with, browsed in the library filled with shelves of tattered books read by past and present volunteers, and had a short visit with the Nepal Peace Corps director. (An aside to this story is that, due to instability brought on by a civil war between a Maoist insurgency and government forces, the Peace Corps withdrew from Nepal in 2004 and has yet to return.)

We left the following morning for Bhairahawa, a southern city near the border of India where Kurt lived and worked. Nepal is a small, mountainous, landlocked country sandwiched between the world's two most populous nations, India and China. Roughly the size and shape of Tennessee, it contains an overpopulated 23 million citizens, most who eke out a living through subsistence agriculture. Our view from the airplane window, enroute to Bhairahawa, verified that making a living would be both arduous and tenuous; sighting a level plot of land was quite rare. The airplane we flew on was an old twin propped affair, piloted, we were told, by an experienced and capable captain. He treated us to more of the majesty of the Himalayas than the flight-anxious Jean could muster enthusiasm for, but we all survived and were elated to touch down at the well-worn but sturdy airport.

Looking at the tiny shacks that lined the streets, we were suddenly confronted with the poverty in Kurt's city. In one such shack was the barbershop where I stopped for a ten-cent shave. The shop itself, no bigger than a closet, opened for business by propping up the wall exposing its humble interior to potential customers. During the shave, I looked down through the floor where the wide cracks allowed me to watch various animals scouring for leftovers.

We stopped at a small English boarding school where Kurt volunteered his time teaching local students. His students would probably remember him for his rendition of "The Yellow Submarine," which was a frequent request. The teachers and students were typically clean cut and enthusiastic about learning.

Kurt worked at a government fish farm where he and a fellow Peace Corps volunteer, Matt, were assigned to assist farmers who were raising fish as an alternative crop (for both economic and nutritional reasons). The hatchery was a frayed, three-storied, concrete building, where moisture issues were evidenced by its water stains and mold. While visiting the hatchery, we met and enjoyed spiced tea with thoughtful and generous people, who shared their meager sustenance with pride.

Kurt told the story of the day he had biked to a village five miles away to meet with a fledgling fish farmer who had requested assistance. Following a day of cultural and ichthyological experiences, the farmer's dinner offer was too tempting to resist. The farmer's graciousness continued after a large rice-themed meal with an invitation (owing to the now lateness of the day) for Kurt to spend the night. Agreeing to the plan, the farmer showed Kurt his mosquito-net-draped bed in one of the two rooms in the simple cement home. Just as Kurt was about to doze off after a long and tiring day, he sensed the mosquito net being lifted. He turned to see the farmer peering in.

"Only one?" the farmer said, as he exhaled his last drag from a cigarette and climbed into bed. Sleep came in short spurts for Kurt that night as he and his bed partner were entertained by a water buffalo that urinated every twenty minutes against the outside wall he was clinging to. I believe the moral of the story was one, have lights on your bike; and two, always sleep on the side of the bed away from the water buffalo.

We had dinner in town one evening at a very nice and modern restaurant, built—it was said—to take advantage of the onslaught of tourists expected through Bhairahawa en route to Buddha's birthplace in nearby Lumbini. We were alone, however, in the large and chilly dining room with a menu void of all but three choices. This was typical as the tourism influx had yet to occur; one couldn't help but wonder if it ever would.

Our walk home from dinner introduced us to refrigerator-sized boxes lining the dark and empty streets. Out of the silence of the night, we heard eerie rustling from one box after another. With a purpose, people began spilling from the cardboard boxes and small sheds they called home. A small, dark shadow emerged. With a shawl wrapped lightly around his head, the villager crouched down to a garbage-fueled fire, rubbing his hands together, seeking warmth. The light cast a glow on the weathered, tired, poverty-stricken face, and the emotionless expression has stayed with me. Suddenly, the seemingly deserted streets came alive. Our voices had alerted the box-dwellers, and we became potential customers. An old man with wares to demonstrate, a young boy with chestnuts to sell—the economy of one Nepali village was stimulated as we bought a trinket or two. We had come face to face with the reality of poverty, an experience we would tuck away in our memory and never forget.

After a few days in Bhairahawa, a driver picked us up in a Jeep to travel to the Royal Chitwan National Park. From the flatlands of the south to the rolling hills of central Nepal, we spent four hours on Nepal's "east-west highway," fording streams and taking in the countryside before arriving at a heavily wooded area surrounded by a meandering river. This would be our home for three days. I felt like I was back in America on a camping trip with my family as I walked among the well-built wooden buildings used for dining and housing. Hearing the elephants' bleating while eating and playing were the only reminders that this was not Minnesota.

After breakfast the next morning, we had to receive an elephant orientation before we were allowed to board the beasts for our jungle tour. During the orientation, volunteers were needed to demonstrate the correct technique of mounting an elephant. Kurt enthusiastically volunteered. He was instructed to face the kneeling elephant and grasp an ear with each hand, then put one of his feet in the curl of the trunk, and presto, he would be hoisted atop the elephant. It didn't turn out exactly as he had hoped as he forgot to turn and thus found himself sitting backward on the elephant, uncomfortably facing the elephant trainer and devoid of any notion of how to gracefully face the entertained spectators. How embarrassing for his family.

There were ten elephants in our group as we headed into jungle grasslands, where we were instructed to look for monkeys, birds, rhinos, and tigers. It was exhilarating to ride on the well-trained animals as they moved ponderously through the park, taking small trees along with them at will. We always felt safe and comfortable on the platform seats mounted on each elephant. On one occasion, Jean dropped her camera lens cap, which the elephant miraculously found in the deep grass and returned by swinging its trunk in our direction and dropping it in our laps. (We had been told they were capable of retrieving items that careless customers dropped, and this incident proved their dependability.) I find that scene hard to believe to this day.

After a short rest back at camp, we were entertained and participated in several Nepali dances. Following a tasty meal, we retreated to one of our cabins. The four of us, plus Matt, Kurt's Peace Corps roommate, had a philosophical talk late into the night about what makes people happy and whether their socio-economic level played a role. I'm certain that this was a chosen pastime for the volunteers. I was sleepy but hesitant about retiring to our cold room, for the temperature had dropped rapidly. One of the best rewards of all time awaited us. A very hot water bottle had been placed in each bed earlier in the evening, which provided a wonderful and restful night of sleep.

Leaving Royal Chitwan National Park to return to Kathmandu offered clear views of the terracing necessary to farm the land. The mountainsides were reshaped and extended where possible, giving the patterned impression of a giant Legoland. Growing crops on land so steep and treacherous is a testimony to the diligence of the Nepali people. The distant sightings of workers thousands of feet above the ground emphasized the severe and rigorous toil of farming in Nepal. From our vantage point, we watched countless people trudge down the mountainside, their backs weighed down with rice straw.

Arriving back in Kathmandu, we noticed that the market district was more tourist-oriented than what was common in Turkey. Turkey was for the Turks while Nepal, as the trekking capital of the world, was a melting pot. The web of streets in Thamel were lined with small shops selling a variety of items, including spices, T-shirts, colorful hand-knit sweaters, Tibetan rugs, statues of Hindu gods and goddesses, art, and a large brimmed felt hat that I purchased to shade my face from the hot sun. Interspersed in the crowds and along the streets were Ghurka soldiers armed and in full uniform.

A major step-climbing workout greeted us as we made our way to the top of the Buddhist Swayambunath Temple. The number of poor people begging on the steps was a depressing sight. The temple spire was adorned with Buddhist prayer flags and Buddha's eyes. Pilgrims and tourists circled the area below, touching the antique brass prayer wheels, while unattended monkeys roamed and perched in random places around the temple grounds.

From the Hindu temple of Pashupatinath, the holiest place in Nepal, we watched cremation ceremonies taking place. The families gathered around the platform where the shrouded remains were laid for the funeral proceedings. It was interesting to note that there were two distinct locations for the cremation rituals: one side of the pier cremation was held for the rich, and the other side for the poorer classes. After the bodies were cremated, the remains were sent down the adjacent unsanitary and polluted waterway on a small raft in hopes of reaching the Ganges River. In the Hindu belief system, the ashes that reached the river would go to heaven.

While surveying the temple, we came upon numerous

people that Kurt described as holy men or *Sadhus*. Small articles for sale surrounded them, and their position appeared to be more ceremonial and commercial than it was spiritual. To play the role of the mystical spiritual leader, they wore colorful robes and had long beards and braided hair that often touched the ground. They were always primed for a handout; sometimes this handout was accompanied by a photo op.

Reflections on Nepal

Kathmandu is a sprawling, low-slung city of tremendous energy. Due to a massive number of people in a small area, don't look to Kathmandu to provide a quiet, structured stay. Any major street corner is in the midst of the frenzied activities of the city. The modes of transportation that whizzed by included bicycles, motor scooters, cars, trucks, their version of taxis, and my favorite, the overcrowded buses where people jutted out of every conceivable opening. Buses were like a merry-go-round ride with poles to grab for those so inclined. People hung precariously on the outside and, when necessary, were carried on top like a piece of luggage.

Everyone seemed to be in a hurry . . . except for the cows, of course.

Our health concerns, thankfully, didn't materialize, as Kurt's substitutionary experience (he had been sick before we arrived) led him to take precautions for us. Both the meds and choosing safe places to eat helped; he steered us away from taking liberties with most street food. An exception was the green rice dish Jennifer and I ate that had been left over from a wedding reception the previous night in Kurt's village. We wanted to show our gratitude and respect for Kurt's hospitable friends. An anxious wait of two days proved that our immune systems were doing their jobs.

As Jean and I talked our last night, we pondered the difficulty of saying good-bye to Kurt. We felt grateful to have had the opportunity to experience Nepal and get a partial glimpse of Kurt's day-to-day activities. Although Kurt lived amidst the poverty of this developing nation, the Peace Corps took good care of its volunteers, leaving us assured that his basic necessities were adequately being met. This stop in our travels had been an unforgettable adventure.

Bangkok

To give justice to a three-day layover in a city like Bangkok requires assistance. We received ours by hiring a driver for a whirlwind tour of the city. On the tour, a gem emporium caught Jean's interest. After much inspection and deliberation of the many jewels filling the cabinets, she bought not one but two rings. Their outcome would be doomed, but that's a story for later. I was intrigued by Tony's Fashion House and the hand-tailored sports coat and dress shirts I still wear today (albeit with a fit that could be described as snug). Our truncated stay was enhanced by walking through the Grand Palace and partici-pating by boat in the frenzy of the water market. The streets outside our hotel were lined with blocks of stands selling goods of plenty. My last effort to stimulate the economy in Bangkok was to have a shave at the airport. It was Jean's idea, and her motivation was not to help the economy but to improve my appearance. I paid $9.90 more than I had for my ten-cent shave in Kurt's village in Nepal.

Singapore

Singapore felt fantasy-like as we lived the life of jet-setters. We were given access to the VIP service in our hotel because of construction in our wing. One right turn outside our hotel room, plus a few more steps, and we were at the entry to a suite of rooms that was to be our second home during our stay.

The VIP room, which was typically empty, had all the

comforts of home as well as two people to serve us. We ate breakfast, read English newspapers, watched TV, and conversed with the staff every morning. After trudging around Singapore like tourists for a full day, we would return to freshen up in time to partake in hot *hors d'oeuvres* and drinks. This substituted for our evening meal on most days.

Everything a person would want to see or do was available outside the hotel or a short bus ride away. Museums, zoos, shopping, movies, restaurants, and a tropical beach gave us five days of an unforgettable vacation.

We had one incident in Singapore, however, that was both embarrassing and unnecessary. When exiting a hotel, we were waved over by a small fellow offering his taxi service to the harbor. The taxi was his bike. Although we were more than skeptical, with repeated urgency he persuaded the three of us to climb aboard his taxi. Jennifer was placed up front and Jean side-straddled the bar between the seat and handlebars. I was told to position myself behind him, sharing his seat. We recklessly went along with this arrangement, and after a few wobbly false starts, we began making our way down the street. As we clasped, gripped, and hung fiercely to our mode of transportation, we began to draw interest from people on the street. Cars started slowing down to get a look at this phenomenon. Those on the sidewalks nudged one another and pointed, amazed by the sight of the oversized Americans being pedaled around town by the slight, small Singaporian.

Weaving by a sidewalk café proved humbling as table after table stopped eating and stared at this circus act parading down the street. All the while, the driver pedaled madly and was near exhaustion. It was the ride of our lives. We reached our destination after a twenty-minute ride.

"That will be $60.00," barked the driver, seemingly second-guessing his decision to embark upon this trip.

I countered with a firm, "No."

We had originally agreed on a price that was significantly

lower, and we knew we were in the process of being duped. We argued, with neither giving ground. Finally, I placed $25.00 on the bike seat, which was still more than the agreed-upon amount. He snatched the money and hurried off.

Returning from a three-week vacation of exotic proportions requires an adjustment that brings us back to reality. We believed that we would make such a transition from the Far East to the Near East easier by attending a camel festival in a village close to Izmir.

TRANSITIONS

The Annual Camel Wrestling Festival

One winter weekend, we journeyed to Selçuk, a village near Ephesus, and the site of the annual Camel Wrestling Festival. I wouldn't say that it was a must-see event, but it was one that you must see to believe. A natural bowl on a grassy spot on the outskirts of the village provided good sight lines for the action. Spectators—predominately middle-aged Turkish men—perched on the hillsides, a cloud of cigarette smoke billowing above them.

The day began with a parade, during which the camels were presented in their finest colors. The marching bands played as the sleepy-looking animals ambled by, oblivious to the music, their handlers leading the way in their turbans and colorful robes. The parade ended and the camels sauntered out of the village to begin the grand march to the wrestling arena. Twenty-some uninterested camels began the trek. I looked for a trait that would give me cause to support a particular beast, but it was difficult to know what embodied a good wrestler. Was it an advantage to have a low center of gravity? How important were the length of the legs? I just didn't know.

Energy and excitement filled the outdoor arena. Several thousand spectators made the action seem like their Super Bowl. This was particularly true for the vendors with their varieties of sausages, cheeses, and figs. More familiar were the customary T-shirts, posters, scarves, and picture souvenirs.

When the show finally started, a handler paraded a female camel front and center for all the male camels to see. At this point two camels and their handlers faced each other from approximately thirty paces. On signal, each handler dragged the camels by their leash toward their opponent with the objective of hooking necks while trying to gain leverage. Each camel then attempted to trip the hind legs, slamming its opponent to the ground. As camel after camel went through the wrestling ritual, I shook my head and asked if I was really watching such a production. Then I asked the inevitable, why? My answer was incomplete in that while I would not travel to Turkey to watch camels wrestle, if I was in the vicinity, why not?

My Almost Daily Walks by the Sea

Old men dressed in the Turkish style—sandals, dark socks, tweed trousers, and patterned shirts covered by dark, tightly woven sport coats—often fished off the esplanade. Their dress also typified their uniform for walking the streets arm-in-arm, sipping tea in the teahouse, or playing backgammon on the streets. Their fishing gear appeared to be as old as they were and consisted of a simple line and a hook and, perhaps, some bait.

On a walk one morning, I saw a father teaching his two young sons how to fish in the Izmir Bay. Their matching soccer T-shirts identified them as young Turkish boys, but their interest and intent in their activity reflected children the world over.

Another morning, along the concrete walkway, a well-dressed middle-aged man huddled over his tangled line. The snarled line would be enough to perplex the most patient of men. Sitting on his haunches he slowly worked at the chaotic mess. Fifty feet away, his wife sat in their green Mercedes, relaxing in her seat with her eyes closed. Her well-jeweled hand held a cigarette. Music followed the smoke out the open window, the rhythmic sounds of a Turkish ballad filling the air. (I don't think it was the Turkish version of "Stand by your Man," but it could have been.)

On one occasion a boy rode by on his bike, using the "no hands" approach, an accomplishment that knows no specific culture. His feat was heightened by the fact that he was riding on a concrete curb about twelve–fourteen inches wide, four feet above the sea. A fall into the water, while not a long drop, would make for a much polluted swim and a bike lost at sea. His hair tousled from the wind, he rode on until a separation or break occurred in his riding ramp. Again and again, he stopped, got off, and remounted his self-styled ramp to continue biking his way around the Izmir Bay. We're talking miles.

One day, turning off the walkway and crossing over to the new footbridge that arched its way across the busy street, I approached five workers who were taking a lunch break. Using the bridge as a table, they had set out a Turkish feast. Their fresh bread, ripe watermelon, green grapes, olive assortment, sliced tomatoes, and bottled water was tempting; I was already a convert to the Turkish buffet. I knew in my heart that they would have asked me to join them had I lingered any longer.

These walks by the sea were critical to my well being. Physically they were a healthy outlet, and from an emotional aspect, they brought some tranquility to a sometimes stressful life. But the most important benefit I received from my daily walks was the closeness I felt to the culture and to the people. Typically, not a word was spoken on my walks, and yet I felt as though I was communicating with them. I could stop and watch a soccer game in the seaside park and learn something about human nature that I didn't know twenty minutes prior. Maybe, too, my presence created something in the lives of those who saw me each day. That I don't know. Somehow I believed that my walks were beneficial to others just as they were to me. But, the reality might be that no one ever noticed me. If they did, the only emotion elicited could have been one of pity for the lonely foreigner who walked the waterfront because he had no life.

Views from Our Balcony

During our first year, a unique Turkish moment happened below our third-floor apartment balcony. The commotion started with loud voices and honking horns, which was not unusual in Turkey. As the racket continued, however, I decided I should take a look. On the street below, a car and large gravel truck faced one another on the narrow street, each unwilling to make a concessionary first move. This standoff completely blocked the intersection. The car, just having turned the corner, had only a short distance to back up to free the way. The truck, on the other hand, had to back up the entire block to find turn-around room. After a few minutes of vehicle nose-to-nose posturing that included more yelling and horn honking, the truck driver jumped out of the truck and onto the street. Many cars were now stacked up behind each vehicle, and I assumed we were in for a fight. The growing crowd watched intently, perhaps hoping that might be the case.

The truck driver, with keys in hand, reached up to lock his truck doors. Without so much as a glance at the car, he walked down the long street in the opposite direction past the line-up of cars behind his truck. The astonished driver of the car watched him walk away while the few cars behind him—blocked and unable to move—resumed honking. With the added pressure of being the lone decision-maker, the stubborn car driver began backing up, while the driverless truck stared him down.

The truck driver, now a block away, peeked around from his corner vantage, viewed the action, and slowly walked back toward his truck. Like an old-time western hero, he had stared down the bad guy and now every one could safely walk the street. The pedestrians stood to the side, quiet but respectful in their mood. From my perch on the balcony above, I silently applauded my new hero for his valiant stand and peaceful solution. He entered his truck and drove off into the night, trailed by a line of cars.

But Things Do Work Out

The reality of overseas living abruptly came to our attention when we received an e-mail from the people renting our home in Minnesota. Due to financial reasons, they declared that they must break their two-year lease and move out on April 30. What was our recourse? Accept that they were being truthful and find a new renter.

Weeks later, Craig, our oldest son, and Heidi, announced they were to be married the summer between our two years in Turkey. A July date had been set and we would all be coming home. Kurt and the Turkey trio had not planned to return to the United States, but by May, we were eager with anticipation. We even had a house to live in while we were home—our own. More good news arrived later through Lynn, our house manager; he had rented our house for the next year. The new renters would move in during the last week in July, by which time we would be off to England and Scotland. Things do work out!

Crunch Time

We received great and unexpected news. Jennifer, after hours of daily study and being tutored to the max, received an A on her math final. That would not be her final grade, but for her it was a major comeback. This was proof that effort is still an attribute and a factor in being successful.

As Jennifer's junior year came to a close, we met with ACI's college counselor and began the process of college applications. She would transfer her Turkish grades to Wayzata, Minnesota, and would receive an American diploma when she graduated. The SAT would be taken in Turkey with other Turks who chose to go to school in the United States. We had some concerns about everything falling into place for her, but there was always uncertainty in most all that we did.

In the final week of school, we learned that we would review the students who had received failing grades. Each failing student would be discussed and analyzed regarding attitude, effort, and personality. Then we would all vote to either pass them or recommend that they repeat the grade. Thinking about all the discussion with the necessity of translating every word made me uneasy, but it was the next task that proved more challenging.

The only activity remaining before summer officially started was a process called average-raising exams. That process is self-explanatory but also disturbing. Yes, a student could raise his or her grade with another test if desired and if allowed by the committee of teachers. I proctored two average-raising exams one day. All students had this option (and second chances can be helpful), but it did breed a mentality of slacking off in the initial class.

The Turkish educational system and some of its policies were not easy to support; specifically, the re-exam-taking policy and subsequent grade changing. But I did defend them at some risk and with a ready willingness to appear foolish. Besides I enjoyed a good argument. This goes back to my main point that we were here by choice and for just a short time. Their programs were in place, and there were some things we should not try to change, even if they were questionable.

Those of us who were foreign teachers and had children as students needed to support and encourage our kids to take responsibility for their own learning and not blame the system for any failure. We had chosen to come, and we needed to adapt to their system. We weren't always successful in that regard.

As the first year came to an end, it appeared to have worn us down some. Living in a different culture had been stimulating but draining. Jennifer, in particular, ended the year having worked harder in school than she had ever imagined. The positive effect was watching her work through problems, using newfound reasoning power. In the past she was inclined to give up or simply say, "I don't get it." But in Turkey, her attitude changed and she learned to sit for hours analyzing a problem and working her formulas. My main concern was that she wanted immediate results and too often her efforts were not rewarded with improved grades. I saw that the benefits would be long-term, however, as I watched her develop into a mature and disciplined student with a passion for learning. Her growth inspired me, and I believed it would put her in good stead in the future.

Jean grew emotionally stronger as the year progressed. She didn't let the small things "get to her" as readily as she had early on. Her computer instruction was a plus as she taught her excited students the rudiments of computer use. The department, however, constantly wrestled with the inevitable technical breakdowns that characterized life in Turkey.

Personally, I was feeling much like I would at the end of a school year back home. The minute-by-minute daily student contact left me a little short on the emotional and physical level. I did lose twenty pounds, which was a bonus, but physically my legs and feet were sore from hours on the hot, hard asphalt and the countless treks up the hills and ruggedly constructed steps of the ACI campus. Mentally, I continued to thrive and be stimulated by the foreign culture. I learned to become more accepting of the problems we encountered in Turkey, both in school and within the culture. I still had a way to go, however.

I had grown some and the changes that preoccupied my life had provided me with a sense of accomplishment and pride, but surely not arrogance, as I had been humbled often. Learning to communicate and overcome the language barriers were major accomplishments. After working through language issues, my years of teaching experience served me well in the classroom. The Turks and our staff were professional and very good teachers. We had fun and we learned. I believe that the strength we gained in our physical education department was a result of our willingness to cooperate, share knowledge, and work as a team.

HALF-TIME

Half-time allows for one's need to take a break, a mid-point in the game. We were at that point in our journey when we needed to pause, assess, and make decisions.

As a family, it felt good to have worked through and solved some of the issues that were thrown our way. Looking back at the beginning of our year, several of the so-called traumas we'd endured appeared quite harmless: So we didn't have a phone for six months. So the water was shut off every afternoon for months. So the curriculum created some problems for Jennifer in math and science. So the basketball season and game schedule were crazy and incompatible with logic. So Jean started the year without any curriculum. These were the events and happenings that made the experience an unforgettable adventure.

I have established that I didn't always handle everything with aplomb and grace. I learned something every single day that will make my future life better. I really believe that to be true. Each day brought a new challenge. It might have been something simple like learning a new word, dealing with frustrations, or the impossible task of attempting to talk on the telephone in Turkish.

Foreign living can be like playing sports. The experience doesn't build more or better character; it reveals the character you have. I came up short many times, usually when I resorted to old habits such as allowing my ego and pride to rule my common sense or replace reasoned judgment. But we learned to cope. Coping is big. *To cope* is to contend, strive, deal with, face, manage, and handle. We attempted them all, and we attempted them every day.

WEDDING BELLS

Jean and Jennifer were both relaxed and even a bit giddy as they packed to go home to Minnesota for Craig and Heidi's wedding. The year's stress and the trials were over and the anticipation of going home was taking over all other feelings. The wedding and the fact that we had not originally planned on returning home during the summer increased our excitement.

We boarded two taxis at 4:00 a.m. Turkish time. The extra taxi was for the fourteen pieces of luggage, too much for the smallish cabs of Turkey. We were taking carpets for friends, other small gifts, the extra clothes needed for the wedding, and articles for our upcoming trip to the U.K.

After an uneventful flight from Izmir to Istanbul, we boarded British Airways in Istanbul to take us to Chicago. It was at this point in the trip that we honored British Airways' request to check a couple of our carry-on pieces of luggage. We, of course, did not know that this would be the last time we would see that luggage, which included Jean's jewelry, along with her rings purchased in Bangkok, some personal keepsakes and financial information, a camera, and other assorted valuables. This disappearance would begin a yearlong effort to get some satisfaction— read: compensation—and the return of our luggage. At the Chicago airport, I dragged bag after bag off the carousel as I waited for number fourteen. We started with fourteen didn't we? I had thirteen bags stacked around me, and I recounted them once again. After a thirty-minute wait, we, along with a dozen fellow travelers, began to fill out the lost luggage form. My stomach burned with waves of anger. This was not good. I didn't realize what losing that piece of luggage would cost me in terms of time and stress, but the accompanying helplessness created more anxiety than necessary. We also did not know which items were in that particular bag and that, in itself, was a process that took over a month to determine.

Arriving at home after a year's absence was a strange but welcome sensation. Friends, Betty and Muril, picked us up at the airport. It was late, around midnight, when we rounded the corner on our street. Jennifer's friends bounded out from their near-by homes, we stopped the car, and she was off to renew life-long friendships after a year away. These friends, their letters, and their calls had all helped Jennifer conquer her loneliness for life in America.

Jean and I entered our house. It was empty of furniture, but full of the memories of our ten years of living there. We were alone in our home in the middle of the night, back in our own culture, feeling uneasy along with the drastic fatigue of twenty-some long hours of travel. Soon I was lying on our mattress on the floor, which would be our bed for the next few weeks; I found it had the same comfort level as the bed we had in Turkey. Welcome home!

I was wide-awake at 2:30 in the morning, after about an hour and a half of sleep. I prowled the house and settled on a short walk. I liked it dark and alone, where I could really feel the strangeness of being home. Interestingly enough, I was not comfortable and was less so the next day, as Jean and I roamed through a Snyder Drugstore buying the items that we had lived without. I kept looking for a familiar face, but there was no one we knew. We both felt like outsiders in our hometown of twenty-five years. How could that be after only a one-year absence?

As we were leaving the store and approaching our car with an armful of goodies, we met the father of one of Kurt's friends.

He greeted us, we talked, and when he mentioned that he hadn't seen us in some time, the realization hit me. Everything here was as it was. Nothing had really changed. We had been gone but were missed by only a few. I know life goes on, but for the very first of many moments to come, I knew that things would not be the same. Something had changed. It must have been me.

The time at home went quickly and well. The wedding, an event that was both fun and memorable, took place on a beautiful July day that was Minnesota at its best. No one enjoyed it more than my mom who danced until her feet hurt. The Novogratz family hosted a celebration that continued a second day with a cruise on Lake Minnetonka, including a band and catered food. Everyone celebrated the special weekend and, as the parents of the groom, we were thrilled.

Our time at home had become a once-in-a-lifetime experience. We vacationed in our own home! And it was a true vacation with eating out, visiting friends, and no worries about the typical. I gladly mowed the lawn, for I knew that I was soon passing on this duty to my new renter, a doctor who was on a one-year sabbatical. Our laziness at home was assisted by the fact that the only furniture we had was the mattress we slept on. And the decision to eat out daily was an easy one, what with no dishes and pot and pans. What an interesting way to live. I have never enjoyed my home more.

ENGLAND AND SCOTLAND

A trip to England and Scotland had been a longtime aspiration for us. We wanted to visit an English-speaking European country, and Jennifer had a strong desire to see Scotland. Her grandmother, my mother, was a full-blooded Scot who regaled Jennifer with stories of the Campbell clan. Jennifer had carried her love of Scotland to an extreme when on her basketball banquet program she was asked to list a hero. While other players picked Michael Jordan and John Stockton as their personal heroes, only one picked Mary Queen of Scots. So, we had our reasons. We would do the usual sightseeing in London and then rent a car to see the countryside.

With a not-so-well-concealed bribe, British Air upgraded us to business class on our way to the United Kingdom. My thinking was that upon landing in London, I would begin my personal quest to gain access to the lost luggage department. I was well-armed with pages of data, letters, and receipts accumulated from my diligent, but previously unsuccessful, recovery attempts.

"Sure, no problem," the information specialist remarked when I asked to check out the lost baggage area at London's Heathrow airport. The lost luggage department turned out to be a hanger-sized area stacked high with thousands of lost bags, many of them sporting the same red ribbons as ours did. And, the regulations prohibited me from looking through the assortment. When I asked the fate of these bags, my host shrugged his shoulders and said, "I believe a salvage company will buy the bags and conduct an auction." This struck me as unacceptable, like a scheme. You lose someone's luggage, toss them a bone, and then sell their luggage? I could not let this drop.

London was the headquarters for British Airways; why not get to know them and devote my spare time to my cause? Maybe Scotland Yard's investigative team was in a slack time of the year and could assist me. I made three visits to the airline office in downtown London, and while we were not on a first-name basis, they eventually came to know the stubborn American by sight. On my second visit, the air conditioner was not working and I became so tired from the heat that I fell asleep in the waiting room . . . or maybe I was drugged. When I awoke, the complaint area was closed and I was shunted out the door. These airlines play rough. I eventually wrote the CEO of British Air to complain and appeal to his sense of consumer relations. This went nowhere, but I persisted.

At the Redland House Hotel in London, we had a small room on the fourth floor—no elevator—with three twin beds with only enough space to walk sideways between them. A sink, a TV hanging from the ceiling, and a window overlooking an alley rounded out the decor. Our toilet and shower were located on various floors above and below our room. The setup wasn't very convenient, but the room was clean and we would be comfortable and safe. Each morning we were served an English breakfast of bacon and eggs with a side of tea and toast.

We loved to walk a new city. Our practice was to hit the sidewalk with both feet because we believed that was the best way to get a feel for a new locale. We'd walk for hours, seeing things not noticeable or appreciated from a bus or taxi window. We continued this practice in London. When we walked out the door of the hotel, we became aware that our neighborhood had familiar sights and smells, much like Turkey. We had inadvertently settled into a Middle Eastern section of the city!

A three-block walk brought us to the renowned Hyde Park with its expanse of trails, lakes, fields of play, and concession stands. A small part of Hyde Park that captured my interest was Speaker's Corner. There you could bring an opinion, hop on a box, and let the debate begin.

In the midst of our treks around London, I took a third trip to British Airlines where my strategy had now moved from recovery to what I might recoup in damages. Locating our luggage was a lost cause, and with dashed hopes, I walked back to our hotel. My mood was now more the result of losing my quest than about losing the luggage. The next day we would leave for the English countryside and Scotland. I tried to get myself emotionally ready to rent a car but wasn't looking forward to the challenge of driving on the "wrong" side of the road.

We left London around noon with a brand new rental. The car had thirteen registered miles. I questioned why the agency would give me a new car; I didn't need the added pressure—and with a straight stick! I would have preferred something old with a few bruises and dents. My troubles began immediately when I struggled to back the car out of its parking stall. Shifting with my left hand was awkward. Manning the steering wheel from the right side of the car was definitely foreign and, in my opinion, should be illegal.

My struggles increased as I became confused and made two wrong exits while circling the roundabouts. My hands were gripping the steering wheel with increased tension as I managed to maneuver the car toward the freeway heading to Oxford. Between awkward jerks and grinding shifts, I silently asked myself what would be wrong with staying in London.

Oxford was impressive and looked more like a sanctuary than a college. The grounds were elegant and the abbey was massive. While touring Christ's College, we talked to an amiable man in the main dining room—a long narrow room furnished with dark wooden plank tables elegantly set for the evening's dinner. The paneled walls were lined with pictures of prominent graduates and educators. This was a location where I surmised many high-brow conversations and debates had taken place over the years. Standing in the courtyard at Oxford made us mindful of some of its famous alumni: William Penn, John Locke, John Wesley, and twelve Prime Ministers.

Chawton was the home of Jane Austen from 1809 until her death in 1817 at the young age of forty-one. On a guided tour of the large charming three-story red brick house, we passed a small writing desk in the corner of her room where Jennifer imagined her favorite Jane Austen books coming to life. Benches were strategically placed on the lawn, and we paused to read and enjoy the backdrop of wild flowers amongst the trees. Before leaving · the area, we stopped at Winchester Cathedral, the burial site of Jane Austen. We were told that she was the last of 1,400 people to be buried inside the cathedral.

The charming village of Chipping Camden was a favorite. Walking down the narrow and winding streets, we delighted in the gingerbread look of the old stone cottages, the gardens with their picturesque flowers, and the sculptured bushes that completed the vista. We romanticized while eating dinner in a venerable old cellar restaurant that this small village would be a place where we could spend the rest of our lives, which is a game we often played.

"The bird bath" incident was unforgettable and literally got our last day in Chipping Camden off to a flying start. A scream resonated from behind the closed bathroom door. Jean shrieked that a bird was in the bathroom and had buzzed her head. I was allowed in as a troubleshooter. The bird had taken an unexpected plunge in Jean's freshly drawn bath. I found a badly shaken woman backed into a corner and a small, frightened bird shivering and shaking its wet wings in the opposite corner. As I reached to snare the bird in my hands, it dived toward the open window. In its haste to exit the chaos, it wedged itself between the screen and a window bracket. Masquerading as the hero, I grabbed the bird by the wing and with a flick of my wrist set it free. My action wasn't worthy of knighthood, but I applauded myself for saving the stricken damsel.

My driving escapades were a daily event. Often-times it was merely pulling out onto an empty street and moving by habit into the right lane, which provoked a shriek from Jennifer, my navigator. As cars bore down on us, a sharp turn to the left lane quickly corrected the situation and my rapid heart palpitations eased.

Roundabouts were also a problem. They are a good concept; it's the process that's troubling. To see one up ahead made me wary, and this discomfort continued as I often slowed down or stopped—both forbidden—or just kept going around and around unable to make a decision. I found it hard to be decisive when my critics heaped their criticism and their directives upon every wrong turn I made. Give me a plain old stop sign any time.

Pulling into the city of Chester one day, I conscientiously patrolled the streets looking for a parking space and ignored the English fellow riding his bicycle on my left. When I finally came upon a vacant space, I became so focused that I forgot all about him and nearly drove him into a parked car. Poor chap, he was in the wrong place at the wrong time with the wrong bloke at the wheel. When I brushed against the side of his bike, he clung to the parked car on his left and yelled, "Eh mon, what the 'ell are ya doin'?" Both shaken, I swerved and missed my parking spot; he composed himself, muttered a few more words, and continued down the street. Self-consciously, I hoped he didn't know we were Americans. Jennifer, seated on the passenger side, was a first-hand witness and was mortified that I would almost run down one of her countrymen.

We arrived in Edinburgh, Scotland, to find the Edinburgh Festival in full swing. The festival attracts thousands of people from around the world who are entertained by artists, street performers, and theater groups in venues throughout the city.

To contemplate finding housing and to separate ourselves from the mass of people, we settled in a spacious park in the midst of the city where a giant stage was being constructed. While we sat resting and leisurely watching, a thundering gang of motorcyclists swooped in to break the quiet. In a matter of minutes, a huge fight broke out between the cyclists and the local thugs. No guns or knives surfaced, but chains and fists were in vogue. We were shocked by the close, intense violence. The police response was prompt, and the situation was quickly resolved. This incident, along with the mob of unruly people, colored our first impression of Edinburgh. As a person of Scottish heritage, I wanted Scotland to be "better" than England. This was not a good start.

A memorable part of any visit to Edinburgh is the sight and magnificence of the Edinburgh Castle. The castle, the oldest surviving building in Edinburgh dating back to the 12th century, hovers protectively over the city and provides views of the countryside for many miles. Two tall brick walls, with an expanse of green grass between them, surround the Castle. Scottish guards dressed in kilts, argyle, spats, and plumes stand at attention.

Having managed to get last-minute tickets to the Military Tattoo, we returned to the Castle to watch an extravaganza of drum and bugle corps from around the world. As the castle lights beamed skyward, even a steady rainfall could not deter from the beauty of the final performance of "Amazing Grace." Things were looking up for Scotland.

Driving from Edinburgh to St. Andrews brought wrong turns and missed signs, allowing us to see many villages that the normal tourist would not visit. Seeing an occasional golf course made my heart beat faster. Arriving in St. Andrews, we searched out the heart of the city to find the local B & Bs. The Johnson method of finding a suitable hotel or motel had been practiced and perfected during the past thirty years. Typically when entering an unfamiliar town, we'd park the car and the family would scatter—all of us, even the young. We would ask for the best rate, check out the room (which eventually would have to pass Jean's cleanliness test), and then we'd meet back at the car.

After comparing notes or taking a second look, we'd make a decision. This time Jean came through with a B & B, run by a young couple from the States, and just two blocks from the Old Course.

Much of our itinerary for Scotland revolved around Jennifer's romantic notions of her ancestry, but we all had some input. St. Andrews was my only required destination. As this was the "home of golf," I merely wanted to walk the grounds and absorb the feeling and history that this course, more than any other course in the world, offered. Playing was a long shot, a flight of the imagination, and not a strong consideration as I hadn't brought clubs, shoes, or golf balls.

While Jean and Jennifer shopped, I walked to the golf center. I rented clubs, ordered a bucket of balls, and hit away. I had been away from golf for a year, and it felt good to swing and work on my game and confidence. There were three courses in St. Andrews from which to choose. Hesitantly, I began walking to the Old Course (1400s). Then, abruptly, I weakened and turned toward the New Course (1800s). While walking, my courage kicked in; I scolded myself for my fearful stance and headed back to the revered Old Course where many British Open Championships have been held and celebrated.

Though not hopeful, I walked up to the starter's shack by the first tee. People normally scheduled tee times months in advance. I tried to look at ease and inconspicuous. Not easy at 6'5", wearing a pair of wrinkled khaki shorts and some rather well-worn sneakers, and carrying an old rental bag. My expectations dwindled with each step, but I peered into the small opening of the starter's shack and asked, "Do you have room for a single today?"

The starter, all powerful in the shack and a bit brusque in his manner, huffed in a thick Scottish brogue, "What's your handicap?"

While trying to decide if it would be better to be high or low, I chose to be truthful. "My handicap is twelve."

His gruff response, "That will be fifty pounds," followed by, "You can join the gentleman on the first green," caused me to gasp.

The feeling was unbelievable! Just like that I was going to play the Old Course. I took two practice swings, hindered by a pounding heart and its swelling in my chest. Miraculously, I hit the ball on the vast, wide fairway. I picked up my old rented clubs, tugged at my wrinkled shorts, and with my sneakers barely touching the ground, bounded down the fairway. I calmed down a bit, hit my second shot to the front of the green, putted out, and hurried to join the threesome, now on the second tee. Two gentlemen from Cincinnati and a man from Michigan, along with their Scottish caddies, welcomed me.

It was the round of my life, but not in terms of score. I hit some shots well and some poorly as the seasoned caddies directed my aim on the oft-hidden and subtle greens. For example, when I was readying myself for a seemingly simple approach shot, Hamish, one of the other golfer's caddies, sidled over and said, "Aim for the left side of the green, about thirty feet left of the pin." I looked at him questionably; his firm and impatient glare, coupled with his statement, "Just do it like I say," helped me make up my mind.

I punched a low, scurrying shot that felt firmly hit, but it had to be off line. Gradually and consistently, however, the ball rolled on and on toward the pin. His ruddy face broke into a smile when the ball stopped several feet from the cup. He then said something that meant the world to me: "Nice shot!" The golf score didn't matter, but I'll always remember the hint and reminder of that day.

Having a pint with the caddies added meaning to the moment as we shared stories of the game of golf and how it had brought us together. Golf continues to give me more enjoyment and sense of accomplishment than anything I do. It's the only thing in my life that I'm better at now than I was twenty or thirty years ago. I also learn more about the intricacies of self from playing golf than any job I've had. Golf reveals and offers immediate comments on the kind of person you are. And, what I have learned has always been telling.

I joined Jean to share my day's news and found that she and Jennifer had a day they felt was par with mine. She asked, "Could we do this again tomorrow? You know, we shop and you golf?"

When would I wake up and the dream end?

The New Course, which was similar in style to the Old Course, was my next day's challenge. I paired up with two Scots, one my age and the other a teenager, and we had a jolly good round. Meeting someone and spending four hours with them in this social setting allows people to learn each other's essential nature—another characteristic of the game of golf.

Meanwhile, Jean and Jennifer had toured the grounds of the University of St. Andrews. Jen concluded that all of her dreams would come true if she could gain acceptance to the University. I was on board with that as I'd heard that the students and families receive golf privileges. Later, on the immense, rolling, putting green we joined dozens of others in a huge social event. Some were serious golfers, and others just wanted to be able to say they'd golfed St. Andrews.

Sadly, we were moving on—our B & B host and hostess fed us, helped us load the car, and gave us a hug before we drove off.

The lochs, the grazing sheep, the Scottish cottages draped in vines, and the fields of heather greeted us on our way to the Isle of Skye. Interesting sidelights in our early travels along this route were the narrow roadways that allowed room for only one car. When another car approached, magically a little "passing area" appeared and one or the other would be able to pull off to let the other car pass. What a practical solution for the lonely and often vacant roads of rural Scotland. Not having to pay attention to what side of the road I should drive on freed my mind to enjoy the surroundings. And thankfully, there were no roundabouts.

We entered the island by way of the Skye Bridge, the gateway connecting the mainland to the island. One of the largest islands in Scotland, the Isle of Skye is renowned for its spectacular scenery, wildlife, and vibrant culture.

We descended a steep drive into the small harbor town of Portree, picturesque with its row of pastel inns. A charming pink inn was our choice and would be our home for the next few days. The harbor was alive with small sailboats, tugboats, motorboats, and canoes, while the dark blue sky was filled with white, fluffy clouds and green majestic mountains hovering in the background. Seagulls treaded the placid water, walked down the sidewalk, or glided by our dormer-styled windows. It would be difficult to imagine a scene more serene, peaceful, and relaxing.

A hike on a trail overlooking the water, and active with other trekkers, proved to be a good workout. When we reached the end of the trail, we rested in the long grass, breathed the fresh air, and reveled in the tranquility of the moment. And we slept a bit.

A special stop for all of us was a visit to the Campbell Castle. The massive building, with four large turrets to secure the structure and keep the common folk away, was also the home to the present owners who lived on the third floor. We toured the Castle and delighted in every nook and cranny. As we looked at the memorabilia in the Castle bookstore, we realized that our ancestors, the Campbells, were not revered. They were tax collectors and vagabonds. I didn't feel good about this discovery, but I rationalized that someone had to take on these roles and duties. I'll bet they were good at it.

When we finally deposited the rental car back in London, the rear tires were bruised and scuffed by my forays with the roundabouts. Yet, though we had driven several thousand kilometers, the car had no noticeable scratches. The fact that I had not struck another car or building must have been destined. I was at peace with the knowledge that for the next year I would use taxis, buses, ferries, airplanes, and trains as my modes of transportation—I would not be driving any cars.

The fact that I cut short our stay in London by a day seems hard to believe as I write this. I wanted to get home (Turkey), and I was apparently tired of one of the world's greatest cities.

Changing our flight was not a problem, but we were aware of the possibility that we could have a one-night layover in Istanbul. My closing argument to Jean was that there were five flights daily from Istanbul to Izmir and something would open up.

Well, it didn't! We spent the entire night in the Istanbul airport watching the night crew scrub the tile floor where we were homesteading. They managed to stretch a half-hour job into five hours, which provided us with our late-night entertainment. Watching over our pieces of luggage and trying to doze and keep from falling off the benches (the kind with the unwanted arm rests) helped pass the night.

One more hassle occurred when we found it necessary to move from the international to the domestic terminal. We grabbed two carts and traversed across streets, a parking lot, curbs, a grassy median, and the stares of many, all to save $5.00.

My decisions were hard to explain then and now, and not a good way to end an exciting summer of travel.

SECOND HALF

We were set to begin our second year. We had learned much the previous year, and we were hopeful that we could apply our knowledge.

For much of my life I had been a "by the seat of my pants" kind of guy, you know, *que sera sera*. I have had to learn how to be more structured and disciplined. I believed that to be a more effective teacher in my second year and to fully contribute and profit from this experience would require a strategy.

Guidelines for year number two:

- Prepare a list of goals that will daily remind me of my quest.

- Develop a mission statement that reads something like, "I will do my best for myself and the people I work with by adapting to the country, culture, customs, and environment."

- Read more about the people and the country's history.

- Learn enough of the language to be respectful of the Turks.

- Practice tolerance with a daily dose of patience. Think twice before responding or reacting.

- Spend more time with the people of Turkey and not just the expatriates.

- Travel some, travel a lot.

SCHOOL DAYS—THAT'LL BE EASY . . . RIGHT?

As we began our second year, the ACI numbers for returning teachers was high. It had only been two months since we'd left ACI for the summer break, but the feeling among returning teachers was upbeat and positive.

The first day of school brought with it a long ceremony of speeches, translations, and presentations of commendations earned the previous spring and summer. The students' enthusiasm was contagious as relationships were renewed and old friends were reunited throughout the day. With eagerness and their usual outgoing nature, they inquired about our life away from school during the summer months.

The feeling of exhilaration seemed at a higher level than I could remember from my previous years of teaching, but as I've stated before, everything is magnified positively or negatively when living abroad. I felt more comfortable, confident, and refreshed after a full summer of travel and vacationing. Standing over those three-foot putts to win a hole notwithstanding, the most stress I had during the summer was driving on the wrong side of the road in England and haggling with British Airlines over my lost luggage.

The first faculty meeting quickly brought me back to reality. The meeting consisted of numerous translations, accompanied by prevailing inattentiveness. I was nominated and elected to represent the faculty as the foreign representative on the LEC, a governing body composed of parents, administrators, and alumni . . . not a significant honor, but an upgrade from last year's membership on the Social Committee. While I never felt that I contributed much to this particular body—and probably should have withdrawn my nomination due to my lack of interest and understanding—it did look good on my résumé.

We moved into a splendid new faculty apartment located right across the street from the school. The facility, coated with yellow stucco siding and white trim, was owned by the school and was a major improvement over our previous apartment. Our living quarters were on the second floor of the four-story building and included a small balcony overlooking the street below. Our two-bedroom home consisted of two floors with a narrow staircase connecting the levels. The soft yellow walls contrasted with the hardwood floors. For lack of a legitimate commercial product, Jean polished the floors with olive oil to bring out the rich chestnut brown color and to clean the dusty surface. We took for granted that the Turks knew of this additional use for olive oil, but for us it was a revelation. The new appliances worked like a charm, and we had a matching sofa and chairs. But we were minus curtains and the workmen had forgotten to build a closet in our bedroom . . . oops. A big plus for Jennifer was a bedroom window, something that she had lacked in our first apartment. All in all, we were thrilled to have such a nice home to begin our second year. Although we felt safe the previous year, an additional perk was twenty-four-hour security provided by the school guards . . . a precaution more than a necessity. We moved the large, black, Russian piano from our old apartment, and Jennifer's Beatles' melodies brought further warmth to our new environs. Two major improvements included no water depots and no quick-moving nighttime bugs.

The communal first floor lounge area was spacious, about the size of our old gym and void of much furniture. We had a pool table that I seldom used, a few books on the shelf, and a TV that worked, but offered only Turkish programs. The ladies occasionally had an exercise class in the lounge area.

One day Jean had this story to tell. An energetic and capable gal was leading the exercise class. She spoke only Turkish, but Jean could easily follow along by watching her demonstrations. On this particular day, the class stretched out on the floor for some static exercises. Jean was not achieving the desired effect from the exercise as the leader called out repeatedly in Turkish, "*Kıstırıldı senin küt, kıstırıldı senin küt.*" Finally, she asked the woman next to her, a bilingual secretary, what the instructor was saying. Between puffs of air she panted in English, "Squeeze your ass, squeeze your ass!" Jean grasped the concept quickly, thanks to the power of translation.

In the beginning of our second year, I was able to participate in my first guidance teacher's meeting. Guidance teachers were chosen to meet with two classes of fifteen students once each week. The purpose of the weekly meetings was to teach the students specific life skills, address any problems, and serve as a pseudo-counselor. The concept looked to be worthwhile and challenging.

My class schedule for the semester indicated that Wednesday was my busiest day. I would be teaching three 80-minute classes. On Tuesdays and Thursdays, I had one class each day, and on Fridays, two classes. The intermittent hours would be filled with department head duties, coaching, LEC representative obligations, responsibilities for the new sports building, and anything else that might crop up during the year.

Every day was different and that was appealing. Each morning, when I awoke, I would first think, "What day is it?" and secondly, "What is my schedule?" It may seem like a small factor to be energized about, but the thrill was probably in response to a fairly regimented six-class-hour day during my previous years of teaching.

At the beginning of the year, we had to attend to *karul*, a process of assessing an Orta student's failure in class. In Turkey, when a student fails, he/she is held back for a year in all classes. The parents could appeal to the legal system for consideration. If the court upheld the appeal, the school then instituted *karul*, the next step in the process. The resolution meeting consisted of the parents, who presented rationale for dismissing the failure, and the student's teachers from the year in question, who defended their action. Remember, one class failure and the student was held back in all classes for the year. After an hour or more of back and forth discussion, we voted to uphold the student's failing grade. My vote to uphold was based on the student's immaturity, not his academic performance.

An early department meeting's agenda for physical education and coaching staff centered on creating a coordinated gym schedule that could be used by all ACI sport teams. This proved to be difficult because the Turkish Ministry had not yet announced sports' seasons or tournament play. The ministry saw the need to change seasons from year to year. For example, our first year the basketball tournament play began in November, and our second year it would be sometime in the spring. This was quite an injustice to the schools and teams, but that was the way it was done. In fact, it was so ludicrous that I was left more frustrated and disbelieving than angry.

This unsettled everyone, which led to the troubled meeting. We talked and translated our way through the department agenda. We argued some, listened a bit, and didn't listen quite a bit. Because of translation issues, I left the meeting with my usual feeling of uncertainty. My head weighed heavily on my shoulders as I made the short trek home. An evening meal at Pizza Roma and a walk on the sea relaxed me and eased the frustration. I was upset and disappointed with myself for letting things bother me that I couldn't control.

When I reflect on my jobs and responsibilities in Turkey, I know that teaching was what I enjoyed most. Working with Prep students required the teacher to be "on" for the entire class period. There was no playtime or activity where you rolled out the ball. Everything revolved around the teacher who was the "sage on the stage," to quote an old adage. These kids had great physical needs, and the small class size and the students' willingness to learn made for an idyllic situation. Tennis, for example, required teaching techniques that included planning, repetition, and hands-on teaching. In the States, this unit would be a quick review, as too many kids who had already had lessons would ask, "Can't we just play?" The teaching situation in Turkey was better.

Since most of the class had never played tennis, we were committed to a slower pace. The tennis unit focused on the fundamentals of the game: balance, footwork, pivoting, and racquet techniques for gripping the forehand and backhand swing. We spent days on the "ready" position, which is an athletic stance: knees bent, weight evenly distributed, head up, and back straight. This position was maintained while the class faced me with racquet in hand. On my command, they turned and stepped forward or took a step backward and pivoted. All the while the racquet was placed in position to strike the ball. The exception was that we were minus a ball for this early instruction. After many lessons, we put the ball in play with lead-up games and activities. This was as close as the students would come to actually playing tennis. There would be a day when the class would be ready to play; I just wouldn't be there to watch.

A secondary goal for all of our classes included a conditioning component. Each unit included running, stretching, and old-style calisthenics for fitness. Because most, if not all, students lived in apartments without a yard, opportunities for play were limited to the streets and the few available parks. The school offered the kids a full range of activities, but their class met only once a week. So, when students were in our trust, we worked them hard to give them the exercise they needed.

A few job-related physical problems began to develop early for me in the second year. That may be a euphemistic statement for "I was getting old." I realized that demonstrating or jumping into a basketball game because the team was a man short was no longer in my best interest. I began to understand why my neck, back, and feet were sore. Though I didn't want to accept my limitations, I limped around the campus at times. A little behavior modification and Extra-Strength Tylenol became my best friends.

Assessment Time

Every few years schools go through a process of evaluating their programs and curriculum. This process is the same for most, if not all, American schools. ACI, however, was connected to both the ECIS (European) and the NECA (New England) accreditation. This meant that students graduating from ACI could partake in curriculums compatible to those required in European and American universities. At ACI, we had been preparing for the evaluation team to visit for two years. The staff was nervous, even though the main work had been done the previous year. This visit was merely a formality. The team of evaluators, made up of selected teachers from around the world, finally arrived at our school to determine if we were teaching the curriculum we purported to teach. We finished the workday, reviewed the assessment information, and plied the evaluation team with a fine feast on the library roof patio. The day was beautiful and the Turks always shined when hosting a party. When in doubt "feed them" seemed to be a successful Turkish philosophy and practice. We "passed" the evaluation.

Jen's Senior Year

We taxied to Roza's Carpet shop where we bought Jennifer a Sumak kilim (carpet) to commemorate her 18th birthday. Determining the quality of carpets involves several procedures. You can turn a carpet over to check for the tightness of the weave; the tighter the weave and the closeness of the knots indicate a higher quality and wear factor. We were also told that natural dyes are preferred over those with modern chemicals. Turkish carpets are known throughout the world for double-knotted carpets versus the single-knotted carpets from Persia and Afghanistan. The color, pattern, et cetera are usually determined by the region they come from or where they're made. Carpet weaving is often a family business but can be studied at a university as a class. For well over a year, Jennifer had been attracted to a particular design depicting an eastern-flavored Noah's Ark. Jen's carpet consisted of a multicolored design of reds, blues, and yellows. Her selection delighted her and has since become a keepsake of her two years in Turkey.

After stopping for an excellent Thai chicken birthday dinner, we returned home and served cake and ice cream to our foreign friends in honor of Jennifer's big day. Around midnight, Jen and I walked over to the campus for a leisurely stroll. Security guards were posted at two of the gates, but it was dark, of course, and scary because of the watch dog with a bad reputation. The dog could be either in a placid (drugged) state or in a vicious, "I'll get you" mood. The rumor was that he was about to be unemployed. Nevertheless, he made evening campus visits highly charged. We neither saw nor heard him as we stalked the steps of ACI. We were thankful for the wonder of modern drugs.

Now a senior in high school, Jennifer had enrolled in a few independent study classes. All history and social study classes, as established by law, were taught only in Turkish; hence her need for independent classes. Two of the bilingual Turkish teachers agreed to set up the classes and then arranged a meeting to explain the course work and discuss her intended readings. A problem arose when neither man showed up at the designated meeting time. Jennifer was upset, and I elected to talk to them about their absence. One of the teachers simply said, "Something came up and I was unable to be there." I was not pleased that both failed to show. To their credit, the teachers were responsible in the days to come. However, the independent study program was not a challenging course of study compared to her science and math classes. Jennifer knew that in going into college the next year, she would be at a disadvantage when measuring up to U.S. standards in English and history. In fact, Jen arrived at college without any knowledge of what a simple thesis statement was, let alone how to write one. She had to quickly learn and went on to become an English major.

Blake House Party

The first school party of the year was at the Blake House, the wonderful restored home that was operated by the alumni. We socialized on the patio accompanied by the light of the moon. A classical guitarist provided the music. The usual eclectic display of food and stimulating conversations made for a superb evening. International teachers have much to share after their summer vacations. We learned of travels to Vietnam, Australia, Cambodia, and, of course, England and Scotland. I continued to find it hard to believe that people lived like this . . . and that included us. It was a world so different from my "other" teaching life where teachers typically worked in the summer, attended summer school, and went to the cabin.

A Third Year?

A meeting had ended and I stood by myself overlooking the campus from atop the library thinking about the fact that I was in Turkey and again wondering why. This favorite mental and emotional exercise of mine continued to energize me.

Our director approached, threw his arm over my shoulder and said, "If you stick around for a third year, I believe we can get this sports building completed."

I wasn't prepared to respond and blurted out something like, "That's my goal," referring to the gym project and not the third year.

Our two-year contract stipulated February as the month to

make a decision regarding signing on for another year. We were leaning toward going home, but in my contemplative mood, I wasn't closing any doors.

Later, my thoughts revisited the idea of teaching a third year in Turkey. Returning might be a mistake for me because I had come to Turkey for the adventure. Now I found myself thinking more pragmatically, such as, we could save a lot of money if we stayed. But staying another year, if it didn't measure up, could affect the experience we'd had in a negative way. I wanted to stay for the right reason. The right reason in my mind would be prolonged excitement, change, and renewal of the mind. Who needed money?

I returned from a convention in the Netherlands with proof that Turkey was now home. In speaking with teachers and attendees at the convention, I found myself saying, "Well, in Turkey we do it this way," or "The problem we have in our school in Turkey is . . ." The United States had become the forgotten piece in the puzzle at the time.

Achievement

One day on the bus, I met three Orta 2 (8th grade) boys coming from their weekend German class. They responded quickly to my question of why they were taking German: "In a few years we will need to speak three languages to get a good job."

How would our American students have responded if they were asked the same question? Were we, in the United States, insulated from the reality of the real world? Were we even aware of the real world? Young Turkish students believed that the world was a global market, and they wanted to be a part of it. Their attitude and perspective on the future was wise and mature. They were under extreme pressure to perform so they could gain admission to the "good" schools and carry out their life plan.

In general, when I asked my students what career they would pursue, a large percentage answered, "Engineering." This response would not likely be the same from an American student.

Two of the boys stepped off the overcrowded bus at their stop; the third boy, Ozan, and I continued our conversation. As Turks squeezed in around us, I realized what a thrill it was for me to be speaking English with my young Turkish student. I wondered about the example he was setting for those close at hand. Granted, our exchange may have done more for U.S. and Turkish relations if I had been speaking to him in Turkish, but that would have been a short conversation.

As our ride was about to end, Ozan said to me in his perfect English, "Can I ask you a question?" Ozan was a very, very capable young man and also quite a confident one. "Mr. Johnson," he went on, "I finished number one in all of Izmir on the math exam last year."

Yes, I know, I thought to myself, you've told me several times.

He continued, "Then why was I only able to get a C on your physical education tennis test last week?"

What could I say? I was not going to leave the question unanswered. "We all have different interests and abilities. Tests in general may not always measure accurately what we really know." As I spoke, it was apparent that he was not buying my explanation. He may have been thinking that the test was a poorly written one. And maybe it was.

I also had interesting conversations with my seventh grade guidance class as we discussed school rules and policies. These students did an excellent job of stating their opinions. Wow, did they have opinions—all given in their second language, English. They were eager to share their thoughts on cafeteria prices (parents' influence noted here), school uniforms and the dress code, and class tardiness. They were vocal and vociferous in their discussion. So much so that later in the day I envisioned them starting a food fight in the café in protest of the prices, ignoring the dress code, and possibly hoisting banners around campus that read, "Stop Ignoring Student Rights!" Nothing happened, but a seed may have been planted.

I had conversations with seniors, former basketball players, who I held in high regard. For a perspective on the life of an ACI senior, consider the following: ten forty-minute periods of class per day, two hours of math tutoring, chemistry, and physics after school, and four hours of *Derşane* (Cram School) on Saturday and Sunday. This student went to bed around midnight and was up at 7:00 the next morning. I understood why he had to quit basketball. This lifestyle was typical of an ACI student, whose social life was limited to an occasional night out, once or twice a month. Drivers license? . . . what for? Job after school? . . . no time. Get in trouble? . . . sorry, too busy.

Turkey's educational system may be lacking in the public sector, but the private school students were being pushed beyond anything I had experienced in the United States. It made me realize we possibly should raise expectations for American students, hold them accountable to a higher standard, and make a degree meaningful, both in high school and college.

Education was of utmost importance at ACI. I observed students being trained or taught how to be leaders. In addition, students took part in a number of service projects, such as spending time with kids at a local orphanage (which Jennifer did), planting trees, and cleaning up parks. There was an expectation from these capable and driven young people that they would use their math and science skills to change the world and to bring Turkey up to par with world leaders.

Those Old Tomatoes Again!

I taught my Prep class students how to throw. In their culture, soccer was their game and, to put it bluntly, they could not throw. It appeared that they had not been exposed to a sport that emphasized the throwing motion. Can I say that they all threw like a girl? Well, this could have been said before the advent of softball and basketball for American girls. Once again, we broke down body movements: feet and body position, including shoulders, arm position, weight transfer, and so on. The students understood the instructions and all became actively involved. Soon, they seemed to have the action down and were beginning to look like athletes.

The next day, however, went terribly wrong. It was a new class, the same lesson, but with different results. Everything was off kilter from the beginning.

Time and again, I found myself pleading, "Please listen," "No, no, no," "Not like that."

I said to Husnu, a student who threw the ball over the fence, "You'll have to sit out if you do that again."

If the lesson wasn't disastrous, it was close. I was like a student teacher in a veteran's body. If I were being observed and evaluated for the lesson, there might have been consequences. But I continued to supervise the lesson and, most importantly, did not overreact.

But I did hear myself say, "Okay, Husnu, sit down!" as I watched another of his errant throws sail over the court fence. I was aided by the fact that the lesson had been successful in a previous class. This class of students learned, just not as much as the other class.

Another low point in class occurred one day when my Prep kids began demanding that I "*smatch*" the basketball. *Smatch* = dunk.

When I ignored them, they persisted. Finally, I said, "No, I can't *smatch*!" And I inserted a comment referring to age.

They all yelled back, "You can!"

Sensing that I was losing the argument, I yelled louder, "I can't!" Eventually, the yelling erupted into screaming. There was no quitting in those Turks! There was no "*smatch*" in this American!

One day I created a scenario for my guidance class. The students role-played a principal, a teacher, and a group of students who were caught vandalizing the school. The purposes of the exercise were to have students take a look at how adults have responsibilities different from their own and to attempt to be objective as they handed out punishment. They were outstanding! Imagination, love of drama, stage presence, and a willingness to perform were the results I received from the class. All who acted were volunteers, and those not chosen were disappointed. I wasn't certain if we accomplished the goals, but we did have a lively, if not entertaining, hour.

Traveling With the Turkish Faculty

We journeyed to Kemalpaşa—a small village in the mountains—with a dozen Turkish teachers. The women on the Turkish faculty organized these weekend events that allowed us to see the rural parts of Turkey. The women were often graduates of ACI, and they had great pride in their school and in their country. The fact that the men—their husbands—were not able to speak English made for an interesting situation as we both attempted to make small talk. I would usually scrutinize my Turkish language manual before these trips to try and impress them with a new phrase or two—usually to no avail.

We traveled up a switchback road until we reached a mountainside café that specialized in fresh fish. Olive trees and fruit trees were common sights, and we could see vineyards off in the distance. The setting was not unlike Napa Valley in its physical appearance, but the history was on the side of the Turks. I mused about the countless years of events, battles, and legends that could be told about this land and what may have occurred under the same trees and on the same paths we were now walking. Turkey's history is truly humbling when I think of the Apostle Paul walking these roads, spreading the gospel of Christ. The lakeside setting, the excellent fish dinner, and the view from the balcony restaurant, which was covered with hanging flowers and vines, made for a gratifying afternoon.

A second trip found us winding up the spiraling roadways

on our way to another mountaintop. The mountainside's terracing also spiraled over the landscape. I was pleased with the bright mint green views compared to the usual brown of arid Izmir.

We settled in at Gölçuk, a small village huddled around Crater Lake—a serene and peaceful site. The village was quiet, for the tourist season had ended. We quickly settled in our rooms and then ventured off on a three-mile walk around the lake. No cars meant no honking—a very quiet and welcome deviation after the long bus ride.

The evening brought time for conversation and a chicken dinner, just like home. The night ended with lively singing and dancing. The Turks are very family oriented, so young and old were present on the dance floor. There are no wallflowers in Turkey, so dancing shoes are a must!

On another fall day, a group of us boarded a large bus for a one-day, two-hour trip to the mountains. A special memory of this trip was the breakfast we had in a small mountain village. The village was a throwback in time as we observed men driving to "town" on their tractors—the main mode of transportation— with their families in tow. Everything, from tractor parts to vegetables, from fruit to hand-made clothes, was for sale at the market.

Our bus parked next to a couple of tractors in front of a small café. A comely, middle-aged woman welcomed us, and we were quickly seated at a long row of tables. How formal. We were expected and had reservations. Newspapers were spread for a tablecloth, and cups of tea were placed here and there to hold the paper down.

Our breakfast treat was *katmer*, a doughy Turkish pastry shaped much like a small pizza. I peaked inside the small bakery/ restaurant to check on the operation and found three women preparing the dough and one man tending the oven. Besides the flour and eggs, there must have been some secret ingredient to produce the wonderful delicacy. I effortlessly ate several. After we were stuffed, they brought out the dessert *katmer*, which was served with sugar and butter as the featured topping. You need to know that I love lefse, and my Scandinavian heritage is important, but for now I say, "Bring on the *katmer*!" The meal was enhanced with six small cups of tea. That is the Turkish way.

The day was not over, for later we traveled higher into the mountains past miles of trees, sloping farmland, herds of sheep, and lazily grazing goats. My memories of that small village remain fresh. The shops were just barely alive with a few items to sell and not many people to purchase them. The ever-present Turkish men, in their tweed suit coats, sat drinking tea and smoking American cigarettes. Occasionally, they engaged in conversations with each other. More often than not, however, they appeared content to sit quietly, gazing off into space. A peaceful time and place.

Frustrations within the Foreign Faculty

I was informed that a phone bill from the previous spring would leave my next check short a few million Turkish lira. It was my understanding—okay, misunderstanding—that the problem had been dealt with earlier. My real complaint was that our check statements were printed in Turkish, which made it very difficult to determine withholdings, deductions, and anything else itemized on the check stub. Shouldn't everything be in English for those who needed to know the specifics, which was all of us? Furthermore, I believed that the foreign faculty coordinator should be responsive to the needs of the foreign faculty and not merely function as a messenger service from the administration. But to be objective and fair, his role could be a no-win situation. He was often caught between complaints from the faculty and memos from the administration. Personally, I saw his role as an advocate for the teachers and asked for a meeting to discuss our concerns. The battle lines were drawn. Well, now I'm exaggerating, for nothing was ever settled in this regard. We had ongoing issues, but those issues seldom rose to the level where either side was unwilling to talk or negotiate.

Later we did have a foreign faculty meeting, which provided an opportunity for a number of us to clear the air. Around the circle we went, each person given the chance to speak about his or her concerns in a healthy way. This meeting pointed out to Joel, our new foreign faculty coordinator, that there were legitimate concerns among the staff. Everything was discussed—from the laundry room schedule, to personal problems, to feeling neglected. My passion came through clearly. I liked the dynamics of a small group of people living in a foreign culture; the challenges were huge and yet fixable. If we stuck together, reasoned things out, and minimized our emotions, we would be able to succeed. It was when problems or situations became all about the individual that the group became disconnected and weakened. In my opinion, by the second year we had gone from a dysfunctional and at times unhealthy (isolated) group to one with improved morale and energy.

Teachers—Whose Responsibility Are They?

An item on the administration agenda was to assess our evaluation system for the school. I considered this a plan that could essentially lead to teachers firing teachers. The evaluation process would relieve the administration from that responsibility and place it on the backs of selected fellow teachers. In other words, teachers would become the bad guys. While strongly believing that teachers should be accountable and fireable, I and others were concerned about this.

A committee was put together to study and propose a new evaluation system for teachers. Publicly it was stated that our task was to create a process that allowed for teachers to be evaluated for the purpose of salary increases and job tenure. I had mixed feelings about being involved, but I also had some strong beliefs and experience, though not expertise, in this area. The Turkish staff was sincere about the process, so I agreed to represent the department heads on the committee. There were five other staff and administrators represented.

Our committee had a series of lengthy discussions on the merits of teacher evaluation, tenure, firing of teachers, and merit pay. These discussions were often passionate, and the participants were enthusiastic and sincere. The current ACI evaluation system functioned in this manner: department heads evaluated their teachers; principals evaluated department heads; and principals were evaluated by the Turkish vice principal. This system had been in place for several years. My fear was that the department head's evaluation would become the critical piece in retaining or firing a teacher. I believe that because principals hire teachers, they should maintain responsibility for their growth and development and, thus, their retention. If the weak teacher does not improve with help, then the principal should make the decision for dismissal. In this way, the principal's stake in the teacher is considerable, they become more aware of what goes on with the teacher in the classroom, and they become the leader of the instructional program. Our committee recommended a compromise: the evaluation of teachers by the department heads should continue, but the principals should be the evaluators for pay increases and retention.

Atatürk's Plan for Success

One blissful day, the 10th of November, the sirens blared at 9:05 a.m. and the country came to a stop, literally. Every year on this day, the nations commemorate the death of Mustafa Kemal Atatürk. Atatürk, the founder of the Turkish republic, was revered as no other man in my experience (even though I believe he made a mistake when he abolished the fez). At ACI, we listened to several befitting speeches, after which the entire school community walked solemnly to the front of the administration building where we placed flowers by his statue.

Atatürk's influence was evident, for later in my two guidance classes, we talked about success. "What is it?" "How do you get it?" Capitalism had spread to Turkey as the typical responses were: "have money," "get a good job," "be rich."

Several Orta 1 students—remember these were only seventh graders—were concerned about ACI's policy of requiring a broad-based curriculum, which would include music and art classes. They were of the opinion that taking classes that would not help them get a good job or help prepare them for the nation-wide university entrance exam were a waste of their time.

Türkçe—Oh That Language

One day our Turkish teacher was unusually happy that Jean and I had done our language homework. She was a loving and sensitive woman with the thankless job of trying to teach me Turkish. She gushed, "*Çok güzel*" and other Turkish words I couldn't understand. It appeared she had been worried that we weren't doing our homework and had given up on us learning the language in our second year. In actuality, we had been doing our homework; and let's just say that learning is easier for some than for others.

Taking Turkish lessons was helpful when we left the campus, for it created harmony and improved relationships with the Turkish people. Most Turks who lived in Izmir did not speak English. Even in the marketplace, English was not commonly spoken. I only wished that I were more proficient in Turkish and that the language came easier. One of my goals during this experience was to become bilingual, which in retrospect I didn't think would be such a big problem. My rationale for my language inadequacy was that we had to speak English while at school, which left little time to practice. This was partially accurate, but it seemed that Jennifer had picked the language up quite well and, to my dismay, always translated when we were out and about at the grocery store, at the bank, on the street, at the market . . . you get the drift. I often lost an opportunity to practice the language as she assertively stepped in with, "Dad, let me help," whenever I became incoherent with my words. Why did she have to roll her eyes and make that tsk sound though?

I had also developed the bad, bad, habit (I'm told) of speaking in kind of a broken English, or if you will, baby talk, when I conversed in English with Turks. My attempts, again I'm told, were not only insulting to them but interfered with their learning. In other words, who wants to learn from someone who talks in incomplete sentences made up of immature voice inflections topped off with a phony accent?

"Vhat . . . iss . . . your . . . name?"

Or, "Vhere . . . you . . . lif?"

I was just trying to be as helpful as a displaced Scandinavian can be.

Need a Scarecrow?

Our director walked up beside me on the flower-laden sidewalk one fall afternoon. He seemed uncomfortable, and after a few awkward pauses said, "Because we're having more discipline problems with students, and because our enrollment has increased the past few years, we need a person to assist the high school dean." He added, "Some people think very highly of you and would like you to consider the offer of assistant high school dean."

If I were interested, the job would start in February when the second semester began. It would become a full-time position the following year. He finished by saying, "Talk it over with Jean, think of any questions you may have, and we'll talk more later in the week."

My first response was strictly emotional and involved ego, pride, and other such human nonsense. You know, thoughts like, "I am the man for the job." My next response, which was more reasoned but still emotional, was an emphatic, "No." Why would I want the aggravation? I liked what I was doing now. Teaching and working with kids was the most enjoyable part of my day.

Attending meetings and more meetings was the most disagreeable part of each day. This decision would be what we call a no-brainer.

The three of us—Jean, Jen, and I—discussed the assistant high school dean position that night. I was surprised when they encouraged me. I became comfortable with my suspicion that Jean had always wanted to be married to a dean. What woman wouldn't?

And Jennifer, she probably believed that it would be more respectable to see her father in a shirt and tie instead of having to point and say, "My dad? He's the one over there in the warm-up pants and sneakers."

With their encouragement, I found myself becoming more interested; the job would be something different and would present an obvious challenge. The fact that I was considering the offer was a surprise to me but then I hadn't said *no* to much since our arrival. You know, cherish the moment, leave nothing on the table, and throw yourself into the experience. My baseline thoughts were that I was flattered to be considered. I believed that I could do the job, but I also felt that there would be regrets.

When I next met with the director about the assistant dean position, our talk was general in nature, until we decided to meet with the Turkish vice principal to talk about specifics. I had not discussed this decision with anyone other than family and was still trying to determine my motivation. How far out of my comfort zone did I wish to be? Was I looking for power? More change? Just between us, I even had the somewhat foolish notion that by accepting this I would be letting my department down. Talk about deluded!

The director, the Turkish vice principal, and I had a candid talk about the assistant high school dean position. I respected the Turkish vice principal very much, valued her opinion, and felt it was important to know how the Turks felt about this job offer. She assured me that the Turkish staff that she had consulted was supportive. I asked if I truly fulfilled their job requirements.

Year Two Apartment Building

Jen's 18th Birthday Kilim

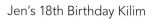

Asim's Brass Shop

Downtown Izmir

PHOTOGRAPHS

Hunting for Olives

View of Izmir Bay from a Restaurant Balcony

Carpet Shopping

Family Dinner at Alumni House

PHOTOGRAPHS

Early Morning Gevrek Run

Lise Computer Class

Physical Education Staff

Father-Daughter ACI Graduation Dance

PHOTOGRAPHS

Final Turkish Haircut

Turkish Men Plus One

Black Sea Shepherd

Final Night on Izmir Bay

They assured me that I was everything they wanted—an over-sized American who could see over olive trees and into class-rooms and not get hurt when he fell. I said, "Yes." It was not about the money.

A short time later, the department heads were having a discussion on behavior at assemblies as students had become more disrespectful, shown disinterest, and talked during presentations. Several people offered solutions.

I listened and finally spoke up. "I have witnessed this behavior before." I paused for effect as heads turned toward me. "What you are describing sounds exactly like our teachers' behavior at a faculty meeting."

Even our director had to laugh. Later someone said, "I thought you were going to say that their behavior was like a student assembly in America."

I chuckled. "Back home, we have basically discontinued assemblies for that same reason."

The high school dean and I continued to discuss the job philosophy and description—I still hadn't formally accepted the position. I knew that I would take the job, but for some reason, I didn't want anyone to know. She voiced her concerns regarding student problems such as tardiness and the students' and teachers' responsibilities for it. I made it clear that I was quite sure I wouldn't be back the next year, but the administration still wanted to give me a go. Any roadblocks I threw up didn't seem to discourage them in the least. A week later, I formally accepted the position.

Little White Lies

Although the following story puts my credibility in question, it needs to be told. Students were continuously asking for ping pong balls to play on the tables located just outside the physical education office. Our policy was that we didn't loan out balls to anyone, ever. Well, one day that all changed when I made an exception for two of my Orta 1 students, Caner and Yiğit. Truly, a couple of characters! Yiğit was the one with the shirt buttons that strained against the pressure from within, which increased daily as he ate and ate. His clothes were usually stained with catsup, mustard, and whatever other condiments were served at the co-op that day. In fact, you had a good idea of the day's menu by taking a peek at Yiğit's shirt. Caner was an accident waiting to happen, and it usually did. One episode, for example, occurred in science lab when he shook up his chemistry experiment and had to be rushed to the doctor for burns around the eyes.

I gave these two boys a ball with the specific instructions, "Don't tell anyone; I will get in big trouble if you do." And again, "Remember, tell no one where you got the ball." I stepped back into the office.

In short order, Kivanç Hanim, one of the physical education teachers, left the office and met up with the boys. I prompted her to ask, "Where did you get the ping pong balls?"

Yiğit stopped in the middle of his next power serve to say confidently, "We got the ball from Caner's mother. She uses this type of ball."

Kivanç remarked, "It looks exactly like the balls we use in physical education class."

Yiğit straightened himself up as best he could, not with pride but with food stains, and looked her directly in the eye. "No, this is Caner's mother's ball, and she is a ping pong champion."

Listening at the door of the office, I smiled perversely. I was so proud of their little white lie. Something told me that this was neither Yiğit's first lie nor his last. I gave the boys an eight for creativity and a ten for loyalty. The story has been our secret until now.

Kurt

It was Christmas of our second year, and we were filled with excitement. Kurt was coming to Turkey. His Peace Corps stint in Nepal was over, and Turkey was the natural place for him to come and stay as our home in Minnesota was occupied until the end of the summer. We were eager to hear a complete assessment of his experience in the Peace Corps. Kurt had also met a friend, Bekah Banks, in Nepal by way of Texas. They had the common bond of working the fishery farms in Nepal and she, too, would stop in Turkey after her travels through Southeast Asia. The aftermath of this story is that Bekah, with her quiet manner and easy smile, won her favor with the three American judges. (Today Kurt and Bekah teach in Singapore and spend summers in Minnesota with their two small children, Hazel and Sam.)

Kurt would make the most of his time in Izmir by teaching English, writing articles for the Turkish Daily News, and determining his future plans.

TIMEOUT—
NEW YEAR'S IN PARIS

Never in my life had I done anything as impulsive and extravagant as our New Year's trip to Paris. We were content to spend the holiday quietly at home until the unexpected happened. (You remember that to expect the unexpected is the norm in Turkey.) We were granted a four-day holiday. We threw caution to the wind and flew to Paris for three days, just like that. Spontaneity and Paris were firsts for us, and we were elated with our decision.

Just before midnight we found ourselves in a small, quaint hotel near the Opera District. We walked into a charming nearby pizzeria, and with a glass of wine, toasted the New Year and our good fortune.

A visit to the Louvre topped our list. The endless line of tourists and the steady downpour of rain didn't deter us. Along with the rain came the wind, which resulted in many umbrellas, including ours, taking on the look of spider webs as they turned inside out and ascended upward. In other words, we got drenched.

The weather improved and after viewing the long line awaiting entrance to the Eiffel Tower, we decided a bottoms-up view was adequate. For divergence we watched young boys from around the world skateboarding in the shadows of the Eiffel Tower. The supple skill and freedom of expression of the skaters were in sharp contrast to the conformity and old world splendor of Notre Dame, the Paris Opera House, and the Musée d'Orsay.

LAYUPS—WIDE OPEN SHOTS

In basketball, the layup is a shot that is taken close to the basket, often uncontested and, as a result, is typically a high percentage shot. It's a shot that the player should make. Coaches are forever reminding players to "make your layups." They are important because against a good team, or in a close game, you won't get many layup attempts. I'm calling this section layups because the stories are short and easy ones; not necessarily critical to the book but, as with basketball, you must take advantage of your opportunities.

A New Year . . . With Drumming

Ramadan arrived shortly after the New Year. During this holy Muslim holiday, the Turks take up "drumming" for the poor. In the middle of the night, men walked around neighborhoods banging the huge drums strapped to their shoulders to awaken their Muslim brothers and sisters. The first year in our Turkish apartment, the men had knocked on our door to ask for money for the poor. We were not inclined to open our door due to the early hour and the unusualness of the practice. The cause was good, but it should have taken place during daytime hours. Maybe they just needed a curfew.

Why? Because . . . Again

One day, I experienced Turkish style bureaucracy at its finest. Kurt had sent a small trunk with some personal items from Nepal to Turkey. To help me obtain the chest, a security guard from school accompanied me to the airport as a translator and a go-between, but he did not speak English.

We started the morning at the Lufthansa cargo facility. There we picked up some forms, and the shuttle race began. Back and forth to various paper shufflers we went. Clerks sat at their barren desks. Stark and depressing surroundings greeted us, a single bulb lighting each room. The dark brown walls begged for brightness and warmth, the setting perfect for a CIA interrogation movie. Nine different people signed, stamped, and clipped on or added to our growing file. I said nothing and followed helplessly as the guard shook his head and smiled with a look that alternated between disbelief and frustration. This shuttling went back and forth for over two hours. There was no waiting in long lines, only delivering our file to another desk. We saw some people twice.

Eventually, I paid someone about $70. We took the final receipt to the keeper of the trunk. He asked me for the key, which, of course, I didn't have. The only logical conclusion we could arrive at was to break the trunk open so he could search the contents. Once opened, he quickly determined that a search was something he did not want to do. The trunk was now mine, and we left the airport three hours after arriving.

My instinct told me that this scene is duplicated in developing countries all over the world. Why, you say? There is only one answer: because.

Volleyballs and Small Bathrooms

At midnight in January, I prepared to leave with the volleyball team to participate in a nationwide tournament. I was going along as a chaperone and faculty representative. My main contribution would probably be to ensure that some English was spoken, since I would be the only non-Turk. We would be traveling to northeastern Turkey to the small steel-producing city of Karabak. Karabak is close to the Black Sea in a mountainous area near the country of Georgia. I had some reservations about going on the trip, but obviously the experience would be worth the effort.

After a fourteen-hour bus ride—through the night and several time zones—we arrived in Safranboğlu, our home for the next few days. The hotel, a 250-year-old converted mansion, exuded charm and a bit of the mystery that surrounded the Ottoman era. The woodwork with its warmth and elaborate carving captivated me; the ceilings were ten-feet high and decorated with intricate hand-carved designs. Each window had an outside shutter, fastened open with a long, antiquated nail. All the rooms differed in their décor. My room had a fireplace with a wooden hearth and a wrought iron poster bed in the center of the small room.

I probably should reveal the negative as well. After the long bus ride, I anxiously wondered about the bathroom and its type of toilet. Much to my discomfort, I passed up several opportunities on the road to use the Turkish-style squat toilets. Thankfully, the commode in the hotel was Western, which I wrongly believed would suit my troubled knees. The problem turned out to be the limited space. At 6'5" and possessing long legs, I found that I couldn't sit on the stool in a normal way. I was required to lift up my knees and jam them into the wall. This meant that my feet were several inches off the floor and my knees were close to eye level. Apparently reading while sitting on the toilet is not a custom in most Turkish bathrooms. You might not be interested to know that while I didn't develop calluses on my knees during my stay, they were sore and took on a reddish hue.

I took a quick, self-led tour through hallways, which were like parlors, decorated with built-in benches, adorned with Turkish carpets, and treated with more intricate woodwork on both the ceilings and windows. The spacious staircase was at least ten feet wide. Our dining area featured large brass trays that served as tables, which surrounded a rectangular pool filled with two to three feet of water. It was here that we ate our breakfast, the boys studied, and we generally "hung out."

This trip was my first experience with students outside the classroom, giving me an opportunity to spend time with Turkish people. I knew only two of the boys, the coach, Sahlattin Bey, and Kadrey Bey, a Turkish teacher/chaperone.

An interesting pattern of communication soon became evident. If I asked a question in English, they would respond in kind. We would then be on the English track and would continue to speak in English. If the conversation started in Turkish, it would continue in Turkish until I wanted in, and so on. I was right; my most valuable contribution to the trip was the fact that my presence encouraged English to be spoken. The boys needed the practice and would not have spoken a word of English without my attendance.

The tournament was attended by a dozen schools representing winning teams from throughout Turkey. I was, I'm sure, the only non Turkish-speaking person in the gym. This bothered me little. In fact, I felt fortunate to be able to enjoy this brief chance to observe the culture in a new setting. The Turks were big on ceremony and pretense, and the tournament was held with that in mind. The vocal crowds seemed to be knowledgeable volleyball fans. Our team played well, then not so well, and, finally, quite badly. Physically and technically, we were as good as anyone, but the tournament atmosphere finally found our weakness; we could not handle the pressure and basically folded from within. That was disappointing and made for a depressing ride out of town. We departed from the hotel on a gray and dismal afternoon. The Karabuk steel mill spewed the foulest brown substance imaginable as we drove past. Snow fell lightly, and we settled in for a long ride home. I was surprised at how badly I felt about our poor play. The players must have been suffering much worse.

About an hour into our trip, the snow increased and began accumulating. I was seated up front on the right side of the small bus when, without warning, something hit us from behind. A car careened off the side of the bus and sped by, ending up in the ditch. A second car was already in the ditch. We managed to stop amidst the commotion of moving vehicles; our driver checked the bus for damage, which was minimal. Several of us walked down the road and discovered that the two cars had not only gone into the ditch but had also hit the same tree. Two men exited one car and appeared to be fine. One person in the first car had tragically died. We were fortunate and had no injuries.

The police arrived, we went to the station where the bus driver took a Breathalyzer test and passed. I thought it would have been more appropriate for the gentlemen who caused the accident to have been tested. After three long hours, we met with the two gentlemen who were in the car that struck our van. They were of Georgian descent and reminded me of how someone might look if they were connected to the Russian Mafia. They both wore black cashmere coats, placed cape-style on their shoulders (I assumed so they could quickly reach their guns). With bushy eyebrows hovering over dark eyes, they did not seem worthy of our trust. My imagination had kicked in.

We all filed into a room in the police station to negotiate a settlement. After about twenty minutes and much haggling, my imaginary Mafia guy, who was most in need of an eyebrow trim, reached into his billfold. The billfold held many bills, but he casually pulled out two crisp, one hundred U.S. dollar bills. He laid them on the table, our bus driver picked them up, and we were off. Insurance? Not necessary if you have money, I guess. We left the police station and walked by their crumpled and totaled BMW as it was being hoisted onto a truck to be hauled away to the Mafia junkyard.

The strange episode left me wondering how much more money exchanged hands between the men and the police.

Personally, I felt that the damage to our bus was worth much more than $200. Most likely our bus driver was influenced by the U.S. dollar that wouldn't lose its value versus the declining Turkish lira. This was enough drama for one evening. We made the safe decision to find a hotel, a meal, and some rest.

With the exception of the accident, the trip had been good. I enjoyed the camaraderie with the players, and they included me as though I was one of the guys. They were respectful, enjoyed each other, and were fun to be around. Watching them play and come unraveled, however, was not fun for any of us. I wondered how I would have dealt with their lack of composure if I were their coach. Perhaps I would have welcomed the challenge because of their talent. My sense was that American boys would be mentally tougher, more composed, less respectful of each other, and possibly a bit looser in their off-the-floor behavior. Were there cultural differences? You bet!

A Missed Layup

When a layup is missed, it is personally embarrassing and often hurtful to the team. It is one of those incidents that should not happen, but it does to everyone who plays the game. I had missed a few layups in Turkey. A critical miss occurred toward the end of our first year. You have heard me speak of the quirkiness of the Turkish curriculum and the fact that a foreign student is at a disadvantage in the classroom with the Turks. Eventually, we sought tutoring help for Jennifer in her math class. The result was an academic version of a rollercoaster ride. One day, Jennifer would come home sad, with a failing score, while the next test she would earn a superb grade. This made no sense. Eventually she began to notice that some of her test preparations and study questions yielded the same questions that were on the actual test. This was where I blew a wide open shot, or as we said in college ball, "I missed a bunny." I finally came to my senses and called a meeting with the math department. With the math teacher and the department head present, I apologized for my inaction and unloaded my frustrations on them. These frustrations included my behavior and that of the math department and the tutor. I concluded the ignoble affair with a long walk and talk with the tutor. You can only learn from your mistakes. Maybe next time, when I get that same shot, I'll make it.

TIMEOUT—ROME,
BARCELONA, CANARY ISLANDS

What could be better than a family trip to a new place to restore and renew one's energy? Because Kurt had finished his Peace Corps service and had joined us in Turkey, the four of us would travel to Rome en route to Barcelona where we would meet Heidi and Craig.

Our first impression of Rome was that it was smaller than we had imagined. We could walk to most sights with the exception of the Vatican. Many buildings appeared nondescript; however, a quick turn around the corner could transform the commonplace into a museum with fountains complete with lounging maidens and water spouts. A quiet street could magically morph into a meeting place for people of all nationalities— some to pay homage and observe, and others to congregate. It seemed paradoxical to find archeological diggings taking place next to modern office construction.

It was after leaving Rome and paying minimal attention to the works of Michelangelo that I read of the man and his God-given drive and compulsion to sculpt and paint. His unyielding dedication affected those who assisted him in the seven years it took him to paint the Sistine Chapel. Realizing the demands he imposed, Michelangelo asked the question, "How many will this work of mine drive mad?"

Staying in downtown Barcelona—La Rambla—was much

like being on the midway at the Minnesota State Fair. A step or two from our hotel, in either direction, put us in front of a performing mime. A glance across the mall-like street revealed a musical trio singing popular songs in English. An artist sat beneath a small shade tree and worked quietly on his portrait of a young girl.

The vibrancy of the street lulled us to complacency. Jean, shopping with her purse strap casually slung over her shoulder, was approached by an elderly, stooped woman. The woman carried a large piece of cardboard that she used to nudge into Jean's side while chattering and pleading for money. While Jean naively began to empathize and focus her attention on the woman and her cardboard shield, the woman's accomplice deftly unzipped her purse from behind. A shout, "Get away from her!" from an observant man (not me) alerted Jean. The two thieves fled for cover in the busy street; Jean zipped up her purse and, with sincere gratitude, thanked her rescuer.

One of Barcelona's most unique landmarks is the Gaudi Cathedral, a structure officially called the Sagrada Família. This unfinished project that began in 1882 isn't scheduled for completion until 2041, approximately 160 years after initiation. The project has been the work of many architects and remains in various stages of construction. The building features eighteen spires and towers, which look like rockets about to be launched. The project is rich in Christian symbolism with the eighteen tall towers representing the twelve Apostles, four Evangelists, the Virgin Mary, and the tallest of all, Jesus Christ.

The plan was to have a few days of sun and relaxation, so we settled on the Canary Islands south of Spain and north of Africa. Craig had promised Heidi a day at the beach. This seemed like a simple request when we packed into our rental car, the smell of sun screen in the air. Our toes anticipated digging into a sandy beach on the Island. Leaving the Tenerife area, we sought our spot in the sun while viewing the mountains and rocky landscape of the volcanic islands. Our aimless driving eventually led to frustration—a beach was nowhere to be found. The mood of the willful travelers changed from hopeful to disagreeable. The petulance gave way to silence, when a wonderful thing happened. We became hungry. We found a small, modest restaurant sitting in an isolated spot that projected into the sea. There we ate seafood and chips as the sea lapped at our table and the seagulls nibbled at our leftovers. The search for a beach continued (we even stopped for directions), but it wasn't to be. Our spirit was not dampened and our will was not broken, but we unanimously agreed it was time to give up. We raced back to our hotel. There is something refreshing about a swimming pool, especially when you can't find a beach on an island.

The windiest of days hindered our attempt at golf. Along the highway, signs were blown over and debris scattered across the roadway. Unlike the beach that wasn't to be, we did find the golf course, but we found it lacking. We were greeted by the remnants of a party, and the club was not even open for business. A young man showed up to take our money and point us to the first tee. We kept the ball low in the wind, and I decided that any time spent with my two sons was meaningful.

Our mood sobered when the family vacation drew to an end. Craig and Heidi waved from the taxi window as they left to return to the United States, and we packed to return to Turkey via Madrid. That it would be six months until we would see them again loomed large in our minds. Living abroad was exciting, but the pain of separation took its toll. (Today, Craig, who works in finance, and his wife, Heidi, live in Chicago with their four children: CJ 8, Campbell 5, Jonas 3, and baby Magnus 6 months.)

BACK TO SCHOOL DAYS

Returning from our vacation for the second semester required some motivation. I had a different feeling as I approached the school, knowing I had a new job and a new responsibility. First of all, I was dressed in a shirt and tie, which probably made Jennifer happy. The fact that I would be working with all new students excited me. As I walked in the school gate, I felt many eyes upon me. Scared? No. Unsure? Yes. And eager to begin again, to prove myself, and with God's help make the most of the situation.

A Job for a Scarecrow

I spent the first two days in meetings to learn the system and some of the problems I would be dealing with in my new position. Introduced as the assistant high school dean to the faculty, I gave a short talk about my reasons for taking the job, as well as my goals for the year. They sounded good to me, but I noticed that I did not receive a standing ovation. I was not nervous but apprehensive, due to the uncertainty around whether or not I wanted this job.

In the beginning, my main contribution was to simply provide the physical presence of a male in the Lise area. Up to this point, most positions of higher authority at ACI were female: the Turkish vice principal, the Lise principal, the Orta principal, and the Prep principal. Just having me around would be helpful.

175

I likened myself to a scarecrow, but eventually I would have to prove my worth, as just standing around wouldn't cut it. I determined that gaining the trust of the teachers might be more difficult than gaining the trust of students, and it might take more time. Neither party really knew me well at this point. I needed to get into the classrooms and to prove myself trustworthy.

The Lise level meeting was held for the purpose of presenting the administration's "late" policy. This was my first attempt as an administrator to advance a cause or promote an idea to the upper level teachers. It went well, as I believed in what was said and proposed. However, I was not experienced in the translation process and struggled with the need to keep my sentences short to enhance the translation. It became evident that I would have to work on and practice developing that technique.

I also addressed my concerns regarding general student behavior, their attention, and the respect they showed for others at the assemblies and flag ceremonies. In turn, I made the teachers aware that they were responsible for the behavior of their students while they were in their jurisdiction. Too many teachers, particularly at the Lise 3 level, brought their students to events and moved off to sit elsewhere. Soon unsupervised students prevailed. My observations and revisions to improve things would be scrutinized and discussed, I was sure.

And the kids—you gotta love 'em. A former Orta student of mine saw me on campus one day and with a huge smile said, "Mr. Johnson, we just love Kemal Bey." Kemal was my replacement in that student's classroom. As he walked away, he made an additional comment, "We miss you though, and we used to love you."

Another boy commented, "I'm both happy and sad; happy for you and sad for me and my class." Generally, it can be said, as life proves over and over, that no one is indispensable. That now included me.

I continued to teach a few Prep physical education classes while taking on the new admin position. On one of those teaching days, we noticed a monkey playing in the trees surrounding our court. The tall trees created a natural habitat as the monkey chattered and swung. Even a fresh banana didn't entice him down from the tree. If the school were in Nepal, the situation would be no big deal, as monkeys were as prevalent as squirrels are in Minnesota. But in Turkey, this monkey sighting was a happening.

Teaching four hours of class brought me quickly back to the realities of teaching life. All administrators at ACI, except our director, taught. As I have said, I believed strongly in that approach. Teaching was typically much more rewarding than administrating. To illustrate, one of my Prep classes—which met only once a week—was to begin a dance unit. Because Turkish students are so outgoing and willing to take risks, when asked if they could do something, they almost always respond, "*Tabii*" (of course). So, we put the students through a few dance steps, put on the tape of "Alley Cat," and turned them loose. Can the Turks dance? *Tabii*.

Teach Well Means . . . ?

As a teacher, you learn each day. One thing I learned in Turkey is that I needed to over-teach if I wanted students to learn. A prerequisite to teaching students in a second language is that you must speak slowly, demonstrate carefully, and model the behavior you want. Then, let the students perform while you observe and give them feedback. Be prepared to adjust the lesson and the method of teaching. There you go . . . Craig Johnson's philosophy on teaching in a foreign country.

Tradition Rules

The Lise principal and I met to discuss our philosophy of discipline. My thoughts centered on establishing boundaries and setting limits for students. After that, my job as an administrator was to assist in making sure that learning took place in the classroom. Conversely, those things that interfered with learning must be dealt with and eliminated. That may sound like jargon, but it is what I believed.

The principal's philosophy was in line with Turkish tradition. That is, the rules were already set in place and tradition commanded they be respected and followed, even when the rules seemed unimportant or unnecessary. Having a partial staff of Western teachers might allow some slippage to creep in and erode Turkish traditions. For example, many of us from the West might have acted embarrassed or sloughed off the practice of students standing when the teacher enters the classroom. The Turkish teachers, however, expected this courtesy. Standing at attention for their national anthem was also demanded. I saw Turkish teachers again and again go up to students at flag raising ceremonies and reprimand them for not standing erect during the anthem. A teacher came to me one day and asked if I would request the director to place his hands at his side instead of clasped behind his back during the anthem. This is the traditional way to stand.

Ties knotted and in place was a practice that some thought insignificant as well. Not to the Turkish faculty.

So I would have to change, for traditions are important in Turkey. I often thought it unnecessary to always have my tie tight to the neck or the shirt tucked in. (Though I did believe that uniforms created a more disciplined and respectful school environment.) I now needed to enforce those rules and focus on what I thought was important as well, such as getting to class on time. You can't learn if you aren't there. Maybe this new job would be interesting after all.

The end of my first week as an administrator approached. All in all, I felt I had accomplished little. All scarecrows must feel like that at first. As a teacher, I had bad weeks but never felt as though I wasn't worthwhile or didn't accomplish something. As earlier stated, my objective was to be seen and make lots of silent observations by merely walking around. So, while I didn't feel very worthwhile, I did do what I set out to do. I guess if you set your sights low enough you will meet the standard. The next week, I determined to talk to more people and be more visible.

I began the week by talking with teachers. The week before, I might have acknowledged them with a wave or a nod, but now I wanted to build trust by asking questions and listening. I asked what they thought the needs of the school were, as well as those of the high school, and what I could do to help. I continued this questioning for a week or two, attempting to learn and build credibility with them.

Yet, I was still a teacher and my guidance class received my well-traveled talk on goal setting. The students responded well and set goals for the future. Because ACI administrators taught classes, the administrator was able to stay connected with what was taking place in the classroom, could relate to the teacher's work life, and could better understand the needs of the students at the base level. My belief was that this practice should be instituted in American schools for the reasons mentioned. Good luck with that!

Time to Shape Up

Not long after starting my new job, I found myself anxious and uptight. This feeling was based on my perception that I was not measuring up to the standards I had set for myself as assistant high school dean. Obviously, I didn't enjoy this feeling. I decided to pick up the pace, take a few risks, and not be concerned with my perception. I developed a plan that would get me into the classroom.

My original and overall goal was to "make it easier for teachers to teach and students to learn." I would accomplish this by:

1. Observing in the classroom in order to reinforce the importance of the learning that was taking place for the students and teachers. (Sound okay?) I had to first get their permission to visit the classroom.

2. Providing a male physical presence in the Lise area between classes and when needed. (Visibility can't hurt, can it?)

3. Attending to the number of tardies that were occurring and helping students prevent problems for themselves with some time management hints. (Good luck!)

4. Acting with integrity and making decisions with the interests of the student in mind. (I would hope so!)

If I lost my job focus over the course of time, I would have my goal sheet to revert to and offer direction.

I was comfortable with and loved the instant feedback a teacher received from students. That is not how it worked in administration where the feedback was not as immediate and it was not as direct and honest. Another side to this administration position was that no one told me what to do. I seemed to be creating my own job description, and I wasn't used to that.

The high school principal and I did meet to discuss and create a new late policy. The real problem was that students were late because teachers were often late. Teachers needed to be in class and ready to begin teaching when the bell rang. Only then could they hold the students accountable for their presence and timeliness. Finally, the administrators must enforce the policies that were agreed upon.

Sound simple? Well, it wasn't, for various reasons. Teachers taught all over the campus and as a result didn't have a "home" room. Their constant movement perpetuated the problem of tardiness. Another problem was the casual approach that the Turkish culture, in my opinion, takes where time is involved. Teachers would tend to get more upset at the looseness of a boy's tie than his tardiness to class. My most difficult task would be to modify behavior, both in teachers and students. Could I do this in a way that was not offensive to their culture?

Climbing Mountains and Dancing Jigs

I found myself climbing up Yamanlar Mountain—a steep mountain not far from ACI—with seventy-two Prep students and other teachers. It was a challenging climb. Most were quite able, but a few had problems. The young Turks once again demonstrated their willingness to look after each other. An example of this occurred when a student turned an ankle halfway to the top; several students gave up the hike to attend to the student's injuries. One of the "helping students" acted like she had a medical degree with her own little first aid kit and take-charge attitude. It may be that they used this as an excuse to halt their hike, but I don't think so. As for me, the hike challenged me and, if my body would hold up, I could see that mountain climbing might be a good hobby.

Testing for the creative Turkish dance unit began for the older kids. This was a first, but with the leadership of the female Turkish teachers, I thought it would only be fair to offer the unit. All the students were taught four basic routines. They were then placed in mixed groups of four or five with the task of designing their own dance. They created a routine, practiced and practiced, and proved to be serious about the project.

In Turkish dancing, the boys have different routines than the girls, so it was their task to arrange their own gender role. Again, the students were amazing in their self-assuredness, and they appeared to be completely comfortable while performing unfamiliar dance steps. What troopers!

We placed the students in their groups around the gym. When a group's number was called, its students moved to the center while the rest remained seated to watch. A Turkish song was initiated and away they went with their creative dance. No one laughed except for me, silently, when the boys went into a tippy-toe, arm-swinging routine. This was in contrast to the characteristically macho style that I had seen in previous dances. I had to avoid eye contact and pretend I was writing. I graded them high for their attitude, for their willingness to try something different, and for their compliance. Their technique needed some work, but who was I to judge Turks doing a Turkish dance?

We finished the session with a vigorous line dance that we had learned earlier. As we were picking up equipment, a small Orta 1 student sidled up to me and announced brightly, "I think I like American line dancing better than Turkish folk dancing." "So do I," I agreed. "So do I."

All of our dance unit classes were a huge success, much more than they had been in America. There were several reasons for this success: it was novel and fun, the teachers did a good job of teaching, the students were motivated to learn, and we held them accountable for their performance with our testing. A student's attitude is always critical when learning is involved, so their poise and desire was a huge factor.

I needed to learn how to portion my time more effectively. I continued to say, "Yes, I can do that, no problem!" This acquiescence did not take into consideration my effectiveness or how much stress it caused in my personal life. Life was interesting, however, for I was able to sit and talk with a new person or two each day, forging new relationships. I was slowly "getting to know" high school students and staff. I was truly fortunate to have the time and flexibility to be involved in a variety of activities.

The Clock Is Ticking

One of my duties was to work with a particular student on his time management, or lack thereof. This student's idea of time management was to know the day of the week. On a typical morning, a campus glance would feature this harried boy with his shirttail dangling, his tie untied, and his hands clutching an armload of books. He managed to do all this while eating a bite of breakfast and running full speed toward a classroom. This behavior happened daily. He was also consistently late with his schoolwork and with his physical presence in class. Yet, he could not see why this was such a big problem to others, namely me.

I told him, "It is a problem because you are here talking to me. It is a problem because of the trouble it creates in your life, such as failing three classes." I continued with the ultimate hammer, "It is a problem because you might not graduate."

He responded that it would help him if all the adults (teachers) in his life back off some. He added, "You need to be less concerned with the fact that I'm late three mornings a week and that I might fail a couple of classes. I'll get my work done. Don't worry."

After more heated discussion, we eventually set up some goals and a plan to achieve them. He wanted to graduate and as he said, "Bring freedom to my life." His English could obviously be improved, so some motivational factors were present. If he graduated, my year would be a success!

I spent several days a week observing and conferencing with teachers. Observing teachers meant that I was in the classroom recording what the teacher said and did. I also recorded what the students were doing, allowing me to give the teacher objective feedback with examples of how they could and did help kids learn. The observations were useful in building trust with the teacher. Plus, we could have a discussion about the particular class and maybe the objective. This was in place of the usual, which was a complaint about a student or the latest administrative decision.

In my early teaching experience, teachers were often evaluated without being observed. How can that be, you say? Well, administrators too often used hearsay, anecdotal evidence gathered when passing by, and feedback from students. Using hearsay and quickie observations to make a judgment, even though the evaluation may be positive, are invalid and an injustice to the profession. My position has always been, "Don't tell me I'm doing a good job without spending time in the classroom watching me teach."

I soon began to notice that my physical presence was reason enough for students and staff to pick up the pace. They saw me, looked at their watch, and broke into a fast walk or run. The teachers' lounge was a trouble spot, as ACI had smokers galore and the lounge was their haven. I didn't enter often, but was close by to remind them of their responsibilities. The message of timeliness was finally being accepted by all concerned.

A secondary benefit of my tenure as a high school dean was the improved physical fitness of both Lise students and staff. In their desire to get to class on time, students and teachers scurried about at a mad pace with an accelerated heart rate. And maybe a few teachers cut down on the number of cigarettes they smoked due to the reduced time spent in the lounge (or in the case of students, in the bathrooms).

The positive side of our concentration on promptness was that the teachers were holding students accountable for being on time. This meant that recorded tardiness among the students was growing in number and the consequences accumulated. I tried to make the punishment valuable and a deterrent for the future. Required study hall appeared to be one of the more successful deterrents for lateness. Add to that a study hall monitor, who was a stickler for holding everyone accountable.

There was a request for me to take part in a citywide dance event. As the protector, or bodyguard, for two busloads of ninth grade girls, I would be an unimportant part of the practice for the May 19th National Holiday. Kemal Atatürk had designated this day to honor youth sports; young people performed synchronized and well-choreographed routines in stadiums throughout Turkey. The dancing was accompanied by colorful streamers, pompoms, loud music, props, and, of course, thousands of dancers and marchers—all girls.

Our kids had practiced at school for several weeks, all at the expense of other activities, including class time. The day was well organized, an impressive display as to what could be accomplished when all concerned were of the same mind. The event proved to be a public relations success, televised throughout Turkey. I questioned its educational value and, in particular, the time lost outside the classroom, but . . .

As we entered the stadium from the parking lot on May 19th, the stands were already brimming with students—all girls, remember—bearing color cards that would later sweep the stadium with a vivid message. The energy bordered on exuberant and the costumes were, by some Western standards, overdone and garish. The precision of the march around the stadium was military-like, so different from the confusion that Turkish life occasionally suggested. Although I didn't understand the context of the program, the ceremony was destined to fulfill the Turkish penchant for pomp. I was proud of the girls' discipline and organization.

Jean's Story

Jean's first-year teaching experience was vastly different from her second year. Knowing in advance that the computer curriculum was quite informal, she brought a suitcase full of materials she had used in the past or had acquired for this purpose. Jean started the first year by writing innumerable custom lessons for both herself and her co-teachers. By the second year, textbooks had been purchased and the curriculum was established.

These lessons were written on her brand new laptop computer purchased just before leaving the States. In addition to the laptop, she had also purchased a portable printer. They both worked like a charm for a few months before the archaic electrical outlets in our apartment literally blew out the power. After numerous trips to the computer repair store where English was not clearly spoken, the laptop and printer managed to limp through the year before she could bring them back to the States for an overhaul.

The rooms in the Science Building where Jean taught her

first-year computer classes turned out to be on the chilly side, and she ended up with frostbite. Her frost-bitten toes were eventually examined in the school infirmary. There the doctor (in name only) on-call was concerned enough to swiftly back his car up to the infirmary door and rush her to a local clinic, only to find the toes passed the test of not being too frozen. She should have followed the example of her co-teacher, who wore her fur-lined winter boots in the classroom.

The second year brought major changes to the Computer Department when it was moved from the Science Building to a new location. Jean's description of the new labs was that they resembled someone's formal dining room instead of a classroom. The walls were a pastel pink, the woodwork was white, and the wood floors, highly polished. As a final touch, the white blinds covering the double hung windows had a pink stripe to coordinate with the walls. She loved the look!

The computer office was conveniently situated between the classrooms. This is where the computer tech person dabbled with programming and did much of his learning on the job. As he spoke only Turkish, he and Jean had a bit of trouble communicating. One example of that arose when she returned from spring break to find he had erased all of her students' completed PowerPoint presentations. When learning of this misfortune, her students, with their unshakable attitude, recreated them without a word of complaint. Jean was the only one bothered by the mishap.

TIMEOUT—
PRAGUE, VIENNA, BUDAPEST

Up until now we had always traveled solo, so we were ready for our first guided tour. Although we would be traveling with twenty Turks, we were assured that our guide would be English speaking. We were also told to watch our valuables at all times in Prague and were given a lecture on precise strategies to avoid the shrewd and lurking pickpockets. Jean placed her purse and camera straps over her neck, just as she was instructed. We hid money in various places. Tour guides told horror stories of how thieves with knives slashed purse straps off the unprepared tourists and how valuables were removed from vulnerable backpacks.

We listened carefully and were determined to be vigilant for the dangers awaiting us. Then, on the first day, while riding a bus, our guide and his assistant, our safety stewards, were robbed of their bags containing $1,000 U.S. dollars, plus a camera. We felt sorry for their loss, but their credibility from that point on diminished.

The cobbled streets, the Old Town Square, the Prague Castle, and the Charles Bridge, with its museum-like stature, all mark Prague as a city to be remembered.

Vienna, on the surface, seemed unscathed from war and revolution. The architecture and buildings portrayed a proper look, very orderly—like there is one way to plan and build a city and this is it. Entering a city by train, however, revealed another side—industry, blight, and a more accurate picture of how people may truly live. The familiar meat, potatoes, and vegetables we consumed at several meals were mindful of Minnesota home cooking. A concert performed to the music of Strauss was accompanied by men and women in historical and authentic costumes. We felt as though the calendar turned back in time as the dancers waltzed around the ballroom floor.

Upon entering the city of Budapest, my mood mirrored the dreary, damp day, but the festive restaurants and entertaining musical shows soon changed my frame of mind. Seated in our u-shaped booth, joined unexpectedly by our school director and his wife, we drank wine and ate entrées advertised as national specialties. Our plates were heaped with sauerkraut and spiced sausages. The dancers twirled from table to table while the fiddlers fiddled. For dessert we drank tea and nibbled on pastries filled with rich chocolate and roasted nuts. I am pleased to say that Budapest's restaurants created more joy and merriment than any we had seen on the entire trip.

The fact that the Danube River divided Budapest into the cities of Buda and Pest, with Pest being the faster growing side, was a revelation. The Danube, with its eight bridges, remains the axis of the city. It was also brought to our attention that our friends the Turks, in the mid-1500s, had a desire to gain power and occupied Hungary for over one hundred years.

What is our preferred style of travel—solo or a guided tour? A tour is more stress free, but you lose your freedom and the ability to go your own way. I missed that freedom. A choice walk to the market is more desirable to me than a forced bus departure at 7:00 a.m. for a tour of a favored castle. In general, when language or safety is an issue, I would consider a tour. Putting those reasons aside, I would choose solo travel and the chance to go my own way, get lost on occasion, and experience the thrill of driving on the wrong side of the road in the unfamiliar countryside.

ANOTHER LAYUP

I talked with three of my players during lunch one day while we watched a pickup soccer game. Two of my basketball players were talented and, in my judgment, they could play at least American Division II ball, if not higher. They understood the importance of a good education and would have been candidates for a scholarship in the United States. In Turkey, students have a choice between the academic route and the athletic path. They couldn't do both. I encouraged them to consider the United States for further education, but it was doubtful they would. Their dreams were not that different than those of American athletes. There was professional basketball in Turkey, but the players normally did not come from academic schools such as ACI.

As we talked and watched the noontime activities, many of my younger students came by to say hi. One of my observant players, Efe, said, "Everyone likes you and thinks you are the best teacher."

I wasn't sure what he meant other than being a popular teacher. I responded, "Some do, some don't."

All three players chimed in, "We don't know of anyone who doesn't think that you are the best teacher at ACI."

I relate this conversation merely because it shows how we often judge teachers—on their popularity. Kids liked me because I tried to make learning fun. This didn't mean that I was a good teacher or a bad one, but by virtue of my popularity with some students the determination had been made. This conversation might also be an example of the advantage an American teacher had. Perhaps, as an American, I was given the benefit of the doubt because I was at ACI for just two years. Anyone can fool someone for that long. Eventually, however, a teacher has to prove his worth and justify the esteem in which he's held.

This type of openness and willingness to express favor was another example of how the Turks could make one feel special and revered. I had never—and from her own experiences, Jean agreed—been more praised, shown more respect, or been made to feel better about myself as a teacher than during my two years in Turkey. The sincerity and the genuine respect that we had been shown would make Turkey an extremely difficult place to leave.

YOU LIKE MEETINGS?
I'LL GIVE YOU MEETINGS.

We suffer through meetings in all cultures, but no one suffers like we did at ACI. The teaching staff was made up of about one-third Turkish-only speakers, one-third English-only speakers, and another third who were bilingual. Every word said at a meeting had to be repeated in each tongue. Think about it. An hour-long meeting became a two-hour meeting. A twenty-minute presentation was an often torturous forty-minute affair. Some teachers suffered more because they were bilingual; they had to listen to everything twice. The majority of us could easily tune out the portions of the meetings that were not in our language—which could lead to daydreaming or visiting with a neighbor, which became another problem. It went something like this:

> "Did I hear right?"
> "Yes, the director proposed that teachers would be asked to serve as last-minute substitute teachers for each other."
> "That's unprofessional. I won't do it. I may have other plans and responsibilities."

Sometimes voices grew louder as anger emerged. That discussion took place in English while the translation continued in Turkish. The Turks typically sat together as did the foreign teachers. Usually I would sit with a foreign teacher or a bilingual Turkish teacher so I could speak with them, if necessary. One group tried to listen as the other side talked about what they had just heard. Conceivably, the bilingual teachers were listening to hear if the message was the same in both languages. The room got louder and chaos sometimes invaded our space.

The translation process also encouraged me to observe body language, facial expressions, and other responses the listener made as they took in a presentation. A simple smile, frown, or squirm by a Turkish teacher could speak volumes. My least favorite reaction was when a Turk began muttering quietly to himself and then the muttering turned to anger as he began venting to his neighbors. I knew then that we were in trouble and the meeting could be a long one.

Meetings could go on for up to three hours. We were all tired after a full day of teaching, and three-hour meetings could cause permanent damage. Normally, I left a meeting with a stomach full of tea and pastries and a head swirling with confusion.

A translator was always necessary due to the fact that what two different parties assumed to be said and understood were often quite disparate. Many meetings closed with, "Does everyone agree?" or "Everyone understand?" or "Is everything clear?" or even, "This is what I heard and know to be true." Very often, what was concluded was completely different from what had been discussed.

I am not speaking only of the Turks. Many evenings I left a meeting confident that I had grasped the purpose and thrust of what took place, only to learn later that I had missed the point. Translating is time-consuming and laborious but necessary. However, the job is not foolproof. I wonder how many wars might have started because a word or two was misunderstood or misspoken as the world powers gathered. The listener is also at the mercy of the translator and must place their trust in that person to be accurate and objective.

A relevant meeting brings unity to any organization. That situation did not often present itself in Turkey. The too-long meetings often ended in a chaotic discussion that moved far from the intended agenda, which resulted in a meeting without purpose or its original intent. We all bore some blame, but causal factors in translation could not be ignored.

What a complicated and difficult job it must be to bring in teachers from all over the world and mesh them into a functional body with tenured Turkish teachers. The administration deserves considerable credit for their tough task.

Over the Edge?

The director mentioned at our full faculty meeting that the School Board was adding a program for grades K–3 and would expect help from the Turkish teachers at ACI. In other words, in their "spare time" Turks would be asked to assist in teaching the lower level grades. Both schools were under the direction of the same board that paid our salaries. I listened quietly, but became angry at the demands.

The moderator called for questions and thoughts from the teachers. The room was quiet. I hesitated, and then finally spoke. "Basically all ACI teachers are working over the recommended load of thirty hours of classroom teaching per week. Asking people 'to do another job' without pay when the salaries of the Turkish teachers are already poor is unconscionable and would hurt their present teaching performance, to say nothing about morale." (The Turkish teachers' pay scale was lower than that of the foreign teachers. Most Turks, at the time, were supplementing their salary by teaching several hours of cram school, plus tutoring, which amounted to seven-day workweeks.)

After venting my feelings, the director retracted some by replying that he was mainly referring to the ACI teachers who had children attending the K–3 School. One such teacher was already working an extra eight hours per week, teaching computers to those students on a volunteer basis. That was her choice, but it took away from the job she was contracted to perform at ACI. As a department head, she had some release time that was to be used for supervisory duty. Now that time was being used to teach at the elementary school.

At this point, I needed to think about my response. Not what I said, but where and how I spoke. Typically, it was worth my time to question myself about my motives and the positions I took.

The first question I needed to ask myself later was, "What business is it of mine?" This was their country and their school.

The second question, "Was I out of line?" Did I speak out of turn, and was I disrespectful with my words or tone?

I remained troubled by my reaction to the director's announcement. I may have overstepped my bounds. I knew that my tone was angry. Was I insubordinate? This situation went back to my original dilemma about teaching in a foreign country. Where did a foreigner draw the line in regard to speaking up about perceived problems? Where did my professional responsibility begin and end? In my case, I had trusted my instincts and my judgment and had made decisions on that basis. In other words, I responded without thinking. It seemed as though I had been there before.

After the meeting ended, I received some feedback that reinforced my short speech. Three Turkish teachers sought me out to say:

> "I liked what you said."
> "Good for you for speaking out."
> "That needed to be said."

Most people, however, said nothing. If they disagreed with my stand, or believed I should have minded my own business, they would not voice their opinion. Most Turkish people did not like confrontation, and I respected that.

The next day I decided to speak with the director, as I

wanted to explain my reasons for speaking out. I was uncomfortable, but felt no need to apologize. I began by saying, "First of all, I disagree with the School Board regarding their expectation that ACI teachers help out at the elementary school on their own time."

He made no attempt to respond, so I continued with, "Secondly, that decision should be a personal one and not mandated."

Still there was no reply, so I proceeded in our one-sided conversation by saying that I was speaking from a teacher's perspective and not from an administrative or school board's viewpoint.

Expanding my remarks, I continued, "As the educational leader of our school, one of your roles is to protect the interests of our students and teachers. By carrying the request and message from the School Board, it looked and sounded like you agreed with them."

I, of course, neglected to mention his responsibility to his Board, particularly if he wanted to keep his job. Speaking of someone who wanted to keep his job . . .

When he finally spoke, he thanked me for coming in and for my interest. He said they would reconsider the proposal and discuss it further with the Board.

My point is that we all need feedback, and at certain times it is prudent to tell a superior what it is you expect from him. The director was very approachable and seemed to listen and put aside any personal feelings that he could easily have held against me. Clearly, one of his strengths as an administrator was his ability to listen to other viewpoints before making a decision. In the future, I would think about withholding my judgment for a private discussion instead of going public. But then again, maybe I wouldn't.

The proposal must have been tabled because that was the last we heard of it. Someone, it seems, made a good decision.

More Meetings

I met with two mothers of ACI students about a program we had instituted the year before regarding weekend sports. The program gave younger students an opportunity for additional free play and instruction in a new sport outside of the school day. It was beneficial for the kids and also gave a teacher the chance to earn some extra money.

The meeting left me in awe of the women and their command of English. Their accent was minimal and their thoughts were expressed well. I presumed that their command of the English language meant that they regularly spoke English at home. Early in our discussion, it became evident that the mothers wanted a format that was different from that of the coach. The coach was one of our physical education teachers, specifically, the volleyball coach. He was interested in coaching weekend sports; he was a good teacher and coach; and he had a strong opinion about the program and its philosophy. He was also looking at this program to enhance the future of his volleyball team. The women were more interested in an intramural approach that would emphasize participation. I began to see that I would play the role of a tiebreaker.

As the mothers were bilingual, the meeting was conducted primarily in English, for my benefit. When they translated for the potential coach, the discussion seemed to become more animated and disagreeable. After an hour and a half of discussion, my concentration began to dwindle. At the close of the meeting, both parties attempted to summarize what we had discussed. What I thought I clearly understood proved not to be true. More discussion followed and uncertainty reigned. The meeting had a familiar ending: "We will have to meet again and talk some more."

This commentary about meetings is not just a criticism, but the reality of the situation when people of different languages seek to hear, to be heard, to understand, and to be understood.

There is no question in my mind concerning my crowning achievement as an administrator in Turkey. It was the day that I conducted a faculty meeting and received feedback such as:

"Craig, thanks a lot. That was great."

"I really appreciate what you did today."

"The best meeting in my three years at ACI."

You ask what great wisdom did I impart? What controversial issue did I solve? Well, I planned, conducted, and achieved the unprecedented—a short meeting.

All fifty or so staff members had settled in for another faculty meeting in the cramped and noisy room. One hundred eyes gazed at me with what I interpreted to be a pleading look of, "Please keep this short." At least that was my hope as I was about to conduct my first full faculty meeting as an administrator. I began the meeting by stating, "My goal is to conclude our business today in thirty minutes." The translator repeated the introduction in Turkish, and by their lack of response, I could see that most teachers were not paying attention. When I sat in their seat facing another three-hour meeting, I usually wasn't paying attention either.

When someone asked a question that was not on the agenda, I deferred it until a later time. When a person became sidetracked, I stepped in and guided them back on task. I encouraged one staff member to, "See me tomorrow about your request." We proceeded this way throughout the meeting until we approached the one-half hour mark. I concluded by saying, "The final item on the agenda is that this meeting is adjourned. Thanks for your help in keeping the meeting short and on schedule. I appreciate it very much."

Most of them sat in stunned silence. Some had not even finished their first cup of tea, and I was closing the meeting. I walked out the door and glanced back to see staff looking at each other in disbelief. Many remained seated while others dutifully began to rise, picking up their materials and foodstuffs.

Even the Lise dean, my boss, was stunned; as my translator,

she wanted the meeting to go on. She stood up and started to talk as people began to walk right by her and out the door. It was awkward, but I persisted that the meeting was over.

Were the compliments I received earlier worthy of praise? No, probably not. But I felt better than I had leaving any meeting since arriving in Turkey . . . including other meetings that I had led. My goal was to have a short meeting and nothing more.

The thinking behind my action was merely to show respect for peoples' time by using it well. When I began coordinating staff development in Minnesota schools, I knew very little about conducting an effective meeting. I had been guilty of running meetings without a purpose, having a poorly designed agenda, and not staying on task. But here, I wanted more. Would my attempt change anything regarding future meetings? Probably not, but at least I made it known that a short meeting was possible and well . . . maybe even a good idea.

We also had issues within the Physical Education Department. Because our ability to communicate was limited, I believed that it was important to have bi-weekly meetings with translation. These meetings, however, were typically hampered by ongoing interruptions. It seemed as though the Turkish teachers were unable to explain to students that we were having a meeting and couldn't be interrupted.

I found it important to establish a few guidelines to make our meetings more efficient and productive. I gave everyone an agenda and a time frame for the meeting. To eliminate the constant outside intrusions, I eventually decided to lock the door to the office and take the phone off the hook. This worked well until the day the Lise dean tried to reach me on the phone. After several calls and still receiving a busy signal, she sent her secretary to locate me. She knocked on the door a number of times; I ignored the knock. The secretary then left after talking to a number of students who were also waiting impatiently outside our door. She reported to the principal that, "Mr. Johnson is in his office, the door is locked, the phone is off the hook, and he won't come out."

I wasn't chastised, but the principal did want an explanation. I explained, she listened, but most likely neither of us completely understood the other's point of view. The significance may have been because our cultures were different and our tolerances and expectations were often in conflict. My justification for my action was, "When I'm in charge, I'll run things as I see fit. When a Turk is in the leadership role, I'll abide by their rules."

MORE LAYUPS

An invitation to a party for two-year-old Belke, the only son of Turkish physical education teacher, Figen, was on our agenda. Jean brought two packages—one a gift for Belke and a second containing some photos to share. Belke spied the packages and naturally wanted both of them. Jean did not want to give up her pictures, so we had a brief struggle between cultures. Belke won as Jean resorted to "eating the grapes," but his winnings were soon discarded when he discovered the contents. A global disturbance was avoided.

The party attendees were mostly Turkish adults, of whom only one spoke English. One of the pleasures of living in another culture is that you're allowed to sit back and watch people interact and not be expected to talk. I was becoming more comfortable with the role of observer. It is surprising how much one can learn about people by watching them and not speaking a word. After a couple of hours, we excused ourselves and moved on to the tail end of another party at the foreign faculty apartment.

Night at Ephesus

Jean accompanied Jennifer and two of her friends to a pan flutist concert at Ephesus. What a setting! Attending a concert in a two-thousand-year-old amphitheater was a tremendous thrill. However, an extra ten-thousand bogus tickets had been distributed, which created a near-panic situation. While Jean and her group were lined up to enter the amphitheater, they were pushed and literally swept off their feet by the extra ten-thousand people, who crowded around them and essentially took over the venue. Jean and Jen's group were frightened about being crushed. Sandaled toes and knees were bruised and scratched as they scrambled up the rough stone benches that circled the amphitheater. Maybe this was reminiscent of the days when the unfortunate ten-thousand wailed and moaned outside, unable to watch their favorite gladiator.

To add to the evening's strangeness, the bus driver, who drove them and thirty others to the concert, fell asleep in the bus and was nowhere to be found after the concert ended. They stood and waited in the middle of a field for an hour and a half, while he peacefully slept. He finally awoke around 2:00 a.m. to begin his search for those he had abandoned. Turkey has come a long way in the last few thousand years, but that evening may have been a setback.

Turkish Carpet Event

A group of us headed downtown for breakfast and a carpet seminar. After the carpet showing—which meant that each carpet was rolled out and displayed for us—there was the hopeful expectation from the owner that we would buy a carpet or two. This all took place at Ali's in the downtown bazaar known as Kemeralti.

Ali had arranged a horseshoe-shaped table for the purpose of serving breakfast in his store. The tables were covered with industrial white paper and the usual fare of tomatoes, olives, cucumbers, and fresh, hot, *pide* bread delivered from an outside source. Every ten minutes, a runner made a fresh delivery. *Pide* is made from dough, eggs, cheese, and topped with butter. It is baked in an oven—think pizza without the tomato sauce—and then eaten with the fingers. The twenty of us, with grease running down our chins, devoured it. Aided by many glasses of tea, I found it difficult to stay awake for the carpet show.

In general, carpet shopping captivated the interest of the foreign teachers and easily became a favorite pursuit of many. The process of buying a carpet meant patience on the part of all involved, both the person purchasing and the men relegated to display all the carpets in the store. However, the first question always asked of the customer when entering the carpet shop was, "Cola or *çay* (tea)?" When the customer was seated—most often on a small stool or perched on a random stack of nearby carpets— the show began. The carpets, usually handled by two Turkish men, were placed on the floor in a long roll and then ceremonially unrolled until they were fully displayed. The stack of carpets became higher and higher and the dust became thicker and thicker. If you were a person with allergic tendencies, the air would be uncomfortable. When all the carpets were displayed, the process was reversed. You indicated which carpets you were interested in and those were pulled from the stack for a second look. Then the bargaining began in earnest.

We didn't buy any carpets that day, but several people did. The seminar was informative, festive, and set the mood for buying. Ali was no fool. Get'em high on tea and Americans would buy anything.

We often traveled to the countryside and watched the women weave their magic, one yarn strand at a time. Even young children sat next to them—usually on the floor—observing and learning the skill. One trip took us to a tiny village where carpets were hung from every house, strung across the narrow streets on rope-like clotheslines, and piled on car tops and in wagons—all for sale. The weaving was laborious and, in our view, made them worth their price. You could buy silk carpets and carpets made from cotton, but Turkey is best known for its wool carpets.

After observing the wide variety of carpet and kilim choices, some of our foreign faculty members decided they would go into business themselves. They purchased dozens with the hope of selling them back home to friends and acquaintances. It was hard to imagine that everyone wouldn't have the same zeal for carpets when we were so intrigued by them. I made a solid attempt to get interested to that level, but most of the carpets I liked did not measure up to what Jean and Jen would consider discriminating taste. And then, of course, my carpet-negotiating skills were parallel with my car-buying techniques, honed from years in the United States. If I want something you have, please tell me the price, and I'll decide right now. I'm an easy mark.

It's a Beautiful Day in the Neighborhood (Göztepe)

The balcony of our second-year apartment provided us a humble view across the street. On a small triangle of land sat a square, concrete building that was both home and workplace to a single family. The flat top of the two-storied building was used for hanging wet clothes, growing flowers, and allowing the dog to roam and bark at the world. The family lived on the second floor. That left the ground floor for the father's work, which was selling fish bait. Each morning, he dragged out a rickety, two-wheeled cart loaded with fish, as interested observers and dozens of neighborhood cats hovered close by. He shuffled around in his sandals with his Bermuda shorts drooping to a length that would have been considered stylish had he lived in the States. He was one of only two older Turks I saw in shorts the two years I lived in Turkey. While shooing the cats away, he chipped ice off a huge block to keep the fish cold.

Similar to many Turkish men, he worked out of his home with little overhead and expense. He shuffled down the street pushing his cart, pulling up his shorts with one hand, chasing the cats away with the other, and somehow keeping the cart moving toward his market destination. Day after day, his life continued in this routine. He received no benefits or pension, probably paid no taxes, and yet provided a service and was representative of what I respected about Turkey—people worked, and worked hard. In our culture, we might have called him unemployed, because he received no regular paycheck. This scene and view is not an "only in Turkey" occurrence but one that I am sure happens around the world.

Typically, weekend mornings began with the loud and piercing call of "*GEVREK*! *GEVREK*!" The sound echoed off the concrete walls of our neighborhood. Initially it was a strange sight to see teenage boys balancing a square board on their head. *Gevrek*, our favorite sesame-coated breakfast roll, was stacked on pegs projecting from the board. The boys walked the streets, calling out to alert interested customers. The young salesmen made their balancing act look simple, but it appeared to be quite a feat. Jennifer insisted that these boys had shorter necks than normal. (She would notice.)

From my balcony, what then happened was magical. The *gevrek* cry elicited the sudden appearance of small baskets dangling from ropes descending from the apartments. The *gevrek* and lira exchange was made and the ropes promptly lifted the morning meal. All this occurred nonverbally and with trust.

Another Turkish moment, and an example of the ingenuity the people possess in that wonderful land, involved a man I often observed. He had an entrepreneurial spirit, selling sports clothes from the hood of his car on the main street of Göztepe, our city neighborhood. The question I contemplated most often was how he managed to get the same parking spot every day. There he was, day after day, with his car diagonally parked and piled with neatly arranged clothes—shorts, shirts, and all the accessories. This mini car market took place on a busy corner, right in front of the appliance store and bank—a prime piece of real estate.

The mystery revealed itself early one morning when I was returning from a *gevrek* run. A taxi pulled up and a familiar-looking gentleman stepped out. Finally I identified him as the clothes sales guy. I stepped aside as he walked to his store (car), opened the trunk, and began arranging his inventory. Apparently, he simply left his car in the same location, providing him the security of a choice spot. As they say in America, a successful business has three requirements: location, location, location.

One Sunday morning, I was up early making a *gevrek* run. I was typically conspicuous in line with my long frame covered in a T-shirt and shorts with the look of a Viking gone bad. Surrounding me were short, dark-haired folks dressed in their old-country look. What must they think of me? I'm sure that some knew that I taught up the street at the American school where none of their children could afford to go. Would they like to ask me about America? Why I wanted to live in Turkey? I so wished that we could sit down outside with a cup of tea and a hot *gevrek* and talk about our lives. I should have brought a translator with me.

With my tall, northern European look, I was an obvious target for the carpet and leather store shills. They saw me coming and called out with the usual come-on lines, "Do you speak English?" "Hello, are you from Denmark . . . Germany . . . Norway . . . America?" or "Do you need a leather coat, cheap?" If I were short and dark, they would have ignored me as just another Turk, but as was, I was fair game for the minor harassment they brought to the shopping experience.

As I was walking through the crowded bazaar one day, another short, dark-haired, olive-skinned tout called out, "Hey, you are taller than me." I didn't think quickly enough for a clever comeback, but it was best to handle those confrontations by ignoring them and continuing to walk. I found that difficult to do. The next best thing for me to say was, "I live and work in Izmir, and I have many carpets and a new leather jacket," which were all true. But they could be persistent and were not easily turned away.

Cultural Exchanges

While we window-shopped in the Hilton Hotel complex one afternoon, a family of five Turks walked toward us. Three of the female members were dressed in traditional attire of long tailored dress coats and headscarves.

"Are you Americans?" the teenage girl meekly asked.

When we replied, "Yes," she beamed and began telling us about her English learning experience. Did I say that she was meek? Her newfound skill was proof to her mother, sister, brother, cousin, and herself as she asked question after question. It was a special moment for us to be a part of this cultural exchange. A newly learned language and the desire to use it motivated her to approach us. Meanwhile, four other Turks working nearby watched and listened to the ten-minute cultural exchange program. We gave each other our phone numbers with a promise to call. I was sure she would.

The importance of this little interchange was the high regard the people of the world placed on the importance of communication and the value of English as a second language. If there is such a thing as a universal language, English would be it. You can travel the world with some comfort, knowing that someone will speak English. The lives of students at ACI changed when they became proficient in English—it created better job opportunities, allowed them to travel more conveniently, and gave them chances to study abroad. To a lesser degree, when our American students learn a second language, their lives are also altered.

I relished the responsibility of being an American and living in Turkey. No matter the circumstance, we were always being observed and judged. Turks are more apt than we are to judge foreigners because we, as Americans, were unique in Turkey. Not many foreigners lived there. I never had this discussion with anyone, but I believe that Turks judged America on how we conducted ourselves, both in school and on the street. I can think of times with our expatriate group—on a bus, in a café— when we would get too loud or say obnoxious things that some Turks could probably understand. But overall we did well.

For a few days while walking to school, I sensed that I was

being "eyed" by two young girls, ten-twelve years old, as they waited to catch their bus to another school. Dressed neatly in school uniforms, their dark hair pulled tightly back, they brightly approached me with the "Good Morning" greeting. The next day brought a bolder approach: "Are you from America?" The following day, from a block away, they waved happily. This went on for several weeks. The visiting was limited, thirty to forty seconds at most, but I'm sure the exchange was brought up in their class and at home, as an example of their use of a newly learned language.

Holiday in Çesme

Jean, Jen, and I celebrated Republic Day in Turkey one spring day by going to Çeşme. We bused the forty-minute trip and arrived in time for the celebration, which included a parade of school children, a band, and a few flag bearers. The school children, all primped and dressed up in school uniforms, were lined up, (typically, I might add) according to height. This was the Turkish way. The smaller and usually younger ones brought up the rear.

After the parade, we hiked the rugged cliffs looking over the Aegean. Then we walked to the village square where we sat at a small outdoor table adjacent to the street and had a quiet cup of tea. The streets were clean and the storefronts spruced up; the setting reminded me of a small town in the United States on the 4th of July.

Since Çeşme is a tourist area, English is commonly spoken. This meant we were able to visit with merchants and have more meaningful conversations than we could in the section of Izmir where we lived, shopped, and worked. We bought a few small items, and Jean had several nice talks with clerks. As for me, I was content to spread goodwill by being a patient shopper—and keeping my mouth closed.

Improving World Peace?

I have a plan to improve world peace: all U.S. politicians, state department employees, and policy makers would be required to spend two years in a foreign country living with the locals. This would not be a Peace Corps encounter, but an opportunity to go abroad to live and work. They would be required to live a life as a typical citizen (not with the comfort and coziness of expatriates) and live without pretense. Upon returning from the two-year "work-study" program, they, hopefully, would have developed a belief system based on firsthand knowledge. Their knowledge would be influenced not just by textbooks, but by a broad-based realistic experience. The ever-popular junkets of today are usually too superficial and manipulative to accomplish that end.

The uniqueness of Turkish culture jumps out at a visitor the moment he or she steps off the plane. In its distinctiveness, it defies cultural stereotypes. When I returned from Turkey, for example, a discussion with friends around the topic of Islam and democracy erupted into an argument.

"Democracy won't work with those radical Muslim people. We are wasting our time and money in the effort," someone said.

Another voice claimed, "You will never see a democratic government in a Muslim country."

I readily pointed out that Turkey was a Muslim country with a functioning democratic government that had been in place for over eighty years. In Turkey, Atatürk was a leader comparable to Washington and Jefferson. As a result of my Turkish experience, I was much more amenable to the idea of the Middle East becoming a democracy.

I realize that I don't know much about the world and its problems, but I do know that these two years taught me about a new culture, which helped me to understand my own culture better. The differences were real and sometimes shocking that first year, but after that, I was merely nudged now and then by the cultural differences.

Here is one such example: for years one of the most important foods in my diet has been peanut butter, which back home I ate every day on my toast. So in our first year, I went so far as to have family bring or send peanut butter to satisfy my taste buds. By the second year, however, the store down the street started carrying Peter Pan peanut butter. Their price of $17 dollars, indicating a hint of black marketing, would not have caused me any hesitation our first year. But by year two, I'd found substitutes for peanut butter in the honey and feta cheese I put on my bread. I was eating like a Turk—and enjoying it. (In the interest of full disclosure, I must confess that today I have three jars of creamy, chunky, and natural peanut butter in my cupboard, but you won't find honey or feta cheese in the fridge.)

Liras, Liras, Liras

Turkey is a cash-oriented society, which simplified my life. The American dollar, which was in short supply, was much preferred over the highly inflationary Turkish lira. When the ATM machine gobbled up my credit/debit card it took me days of finagling to get it back. And that made it easier to go with the system and use cash.

Balancing my two checking accounts while in Turkey was always a challenge. Inflation was said to run about 100% per year and, as the government kept adding zeros to the denominations, we had currency notes of 250,000 and 500,000 liras that equated to but a few dollars. We were also told that our salaries were adjusted periodically to account for the inflation. I took their word for it.

I had two ATM cards—one for an account in the United States and the second with a bank in Turkey. My school check was deposited in the Turkish bank. I deposited my pension money in my U.S. account and received my statement about six weeks later. Consequently, because one account lost value daily and the other was far from being current, I never really knew how much money I had. Was this a problem? It could have been, but as I said earlier, money seemed to have less meaning for me in Turkey. For example, one day I found over $600 I had hidden in the pocket of a seldom-worn suit coat. It certainly improved my day, but not in the same way that it would have back home. There it would have been cause for celebration!

Otherwise, my bookkeeping was a breeze since I had only one bill to pay each month—the phone bill. Every month, I walked about five blocks from the school through a neighborhood of shops and apartment complexes where I opened a gate and walked across a yard with uncommon patches of grass. It may even have been a private yard. The small sign indicated my designation. Not being certain what I owed, I passed the statement under the opening in the glass and strained to understand when they gave me a figure of millions of Turkish lira. I always brought lots of money and began to carefully lay out the big bills. Eventually the teller lost patience in my approach, grabbed the small pile, and took what she needed (wanted?). I was encouraged that there was always something left over.

Crank Johnson?

After an excellent dinner of fresh sea bass one evening, I tipped the waiter generously. He appreciated it and asked my name. He repeated, "Crank," and I said, "No, Craig." He followed up with another "Crank." Now I knew how the Turkish students felt when I mispronounced their names. "It's not Mehmet; it's pronounced Meh-met," the exasperated student reminded me daily. I found that if I exhaled through my nose when I said the name, it sounded more Turkish. Try it . . . Mmmeh . . . Mmmet.

Logic

While riding the bus one day, I sat with a young ACI student. We began talking about travel and eventually foreign food.

Can said, "Most Turks don't like Asian food." In fact, he maintained, "The majority of Turks traveling to Asia bring their own food with them."

"Really," I said. "I didn't know that."

If what he said was true about the Turks' opinion of Asian food, I decided that I would be an advocate for Asian food and said, "Their food must be very healthy though because you don't see many fat people from Asia."

He gave me a quick turn of the head and retorted, "Maybe they don't like to eat their own food either."

Good logic. I could only smile in return.

Garbage Toss

On a bus ride downtown, a middle-aged man sitting in a front seat moved across the aisle and, with a quick flick of the wrist, tossed his empty plastic water bottle out the window. The bottle tumbled and rolled to a stop on the grass boulevard, and a feeling of disgust surged through my body. I was offended! I looked to others for some sort of reaction but didn't see any. I sat back in my seat, took a deep breath, and tried to relax. We do litter in the States, but it had been twenty years since I had seen such an open example.

On another occasion while walking by the sea, we witnessed a much worse example of pollution. On this particular day, Jean and I were enjoying the view but trying not to breathe too deeply, to prevent the water's odor from invading our sinuses. Just ahead of us, a small, bearded man of about thirty picked up an over-flowing trash can and walked toward the water. What was he doing? We were astonished and repulsed as he dumped the entire contents into the bay and then replaced the empty container in its original spot. He was as casual as if he were bringing a garbage bag out to the curb.

The pollution problem is grave regarding the Aegean Sea. So much so that, supposedly, a Japanese company offered to clean the harbor without charge—a multi-million dollar endeavor. All they asked for in return were the rights to any and all findings on the bottom of the sea, as ruins are everywhere. Turkey said no, that they had other concerns, and this was not a priority. My response was that, at a minimum, the pollution should be stopped. Clean up could happen later, but proper education of the people and the enforcement of an anti-litter policy was in order. The man we had just watched needed to be in the front row of that no-littering class.

Asim's Copper Shop

Asim's Copper Shop—a hole-in-the-wall store, close to the heart of downtown—was one of our favorite shopping hangouts. Asim was a sweet man who spoke excellent English. We shopped leisurely and were never pressured to buy. His college professor look, complete with a cardigan sweater over shirt and tie, and a disposition like the Avon lady, made him a formidable salesman who would let us take anything home to try it out.

"No problem, no problem," was Asim's ready response when we said, "I am not sure if this will fit in."

"You take home. No problem, no problem."

When questioned about a scratch or the quirkiness of a piece, Asim was quick to respond, "I will take this to my work-shop and my men will make it better." On one occasion, Asim loaded us and another couple in his car and drove us home, as we were laden with copper and brass. Oh yes, the shop was a mess in any language. Only Asim knew under which pile a candleholder or Ottoman lunch pail could be found.

An added benefit of the shopping experience was the hand-washing ritual. There was never an occasion when our hands were not literally black with dirt and residue after touching and examining each and every one of our favorite copper and brass items. We accommodated Asim when he asked us to hold out our hands, while he poured water from a large glass water jug positioned right outside the front door. We rubbed our hands together to loosen the dirt and then repeated the process a couple of times before our hands were washed clean. I'm sure this routine was repeated with every customer.

Cross-Cultural Concerns

The three of us were invited to lunch at the home of Jennifer's friend, Kayra. Her mother was English and her father Turkish. The children were raised in Turkey but spoke excellent English, all with a British accent. Our afternoon conversation centered on their upcoming visit to the United States—perhaps the main reason we'd been invited to lunch. They expressed genuine concern about the violence in America.

Pointedly they asked, "What is the risk of driving from Phoenix to Dallas?"

What had disturbed them was a newspaper article about carjacking and the kidnapping of foreigners driving rental cars. The gun violence in America was also well reported in Turkey, so their concerns may have been warranted. Their worries also pointed out the stereotypes we embrace from nothing more than hearsay from TV shows or a slanted news article. As an American, I was bothered by the reports.

Our advice to Jen's friend and their family was, "Go to America, plan your trip well, and enjoy the drive."

Not to give them something else to worry about, I said, "The danger of your air-conditioner conking out on a desert road is a much greater health risk than being kidnapped." Besides, their excellent English alone reduced their susceptibility to danger.

Being a traveler in a foreign land makes a person more vulnerable because of the need to rely on others for directions,

recommendations, logistics, and so forth. Our first consider-
ations on coming to Turkey also involved safety. As I have cited
before, we felt as safe, or often times safer, in our travels in Turkey
and elsewhere than we did when in the United States. We also
felt free from worry with Jennifer moving about in Izmir, a city
of over three million people. This led to her taking a taxi a time
or two to meet someone, or a solo ride on the bus to meet her
tutor. Driving on the cross-country highways appeared to be,
without doubt, the most dangerous activity that one could
engage in while in Turkey.

Jennifer—College Bound

The news of the day—Jennifer A. Johnson had been accepted to
the University of St. Andrews in Scotland. While the foreign
faculty was celebrating St. Patrick's Day at the apartment, I had
slipped away to the campus to pick up the mail. This was still a
highlight for me, because I was so surprised that letters and
magazines actually reached their destination. I was hopeful that
the thickness of the package from St. Andrews was an indication
of acceptance, and I was right. Everyone, about twenty partiers,
reveled in the moment. I was most proud of the fact that this
acceptance was accomplished through Jen's dedication and
effort. God had blessed her with certain abilities. She had put
them to good use.

Jennifer soon heard from all the schools she had sent applications to except the University of Virginia. She had been
accepted at St. Andrews in Scotland, St. Olaf in Minnesota, and
the University of New Hampshire. She had been wait-listed at
Macalester and rejected at Grinnell. She was a bit wounded,
feeling the pain of her first rejection. It helped her, however, to
learn that Grinnell accepted only 340 out of 2,800 applicants.

If Virginia came through, she would have terrific schools
from which to choose. Assuming that the academic challenges of
the education she would receive both home and abroad were

similar, Jennifer leaned toward UVa, based on the belief that an American education would provide more out-of-the-classroom learning. The exposure and opportunities to join clubs, music groups, lectures, and sports, would be greater in the American system than in Europe (St. Andrews). At least that was what we all believed.

A month later, Jennifer finally received her acceptance from the University of Virginia. Yeah!! Jean and I both agreed that the decision was Jen's to make, so our role was to listen and offer advice when asked. When we got home to Minneapolis that summer, she would only have three weeks to get ready for college. Not much time.

The reason for the delay in Jennifer's acceptance to UVa was because part one of the two-part application process was lost between Izmir and Charlottesville. This delay caused both apprehension for the applicant and confusion that led to UVa thinking Jen was a foreign student. (Somewhere in the world there may be a Turk named Jennifer Johnson, but I doubt it.)

IT'S A BALL

My second year as coach brought a new combination that included eight sophmores (Lise 1) out of an eleven-man team. Even though we were young, the potential was there for a good team. The team's attitude was different than that of my first year, for the students appeared to be more focused on basketball. Potentially, this focus would make practices more productive and meaningful. We talked about fitting basketball into their tightly wound academic world, and I emphasized that they should have a two-fold purpose—be good in the classroom and on the basketball court. These players resembled American kids in respect to the high value they placed on playing, especially since they were not seniors.

In our first several practices, I broke the team into groups of four, allowing me to emphasize individual fundamentals. Offensively we worked on screening, setting up your man properly, and floor spacing. On defense we stressed communicating with their teammates, fighting through screens, and something called help and recover. Each player received hands-on coaching with few distractions. The players' attitudes were good. They were not concerned with how many points they made or the macho attitude of who defeated whom in a one-on-one match. We needed to practice (do our homework) before we played (took the test). I enjoyed this kind of practice and so did the players. In my opinion, we would have a good team, due to their ability, motivation, and interest in the game.

The team possessed above-average talent: two 6'5" players, three 6'2" players, and two 5'11" guards exhibiting quickness and hustle. Outside shooting—meaning shooting long shots— was our weakness, and we had to find ways to compensate. Mainly, I liked their attitude, their willingness to listen, and their hustle. A typical practice ended with the players pleading, "Let's have one more match (scrimmage)."

Kids around the world plead to play basketball, but they must practice the skills of the game in order to play well. A complete player knows how to move without the ball, how to stop his opponent, and how to gain position for successful rebounding, in addition to shooting, passing, and dribbling.

The shooting game "lightning" marked the end of our established practices. With typical Turkish frenzy, the game became much more than it really was. What an enjoyable team to coach—and one that would require me to match their enthusiasm and motivation!

We worked on shooting-off-the-pass, running our fast-breaks, and denying the ball on defense. The boys' fundamentals improved as they worked harder and concentrated better. We ended one practice with a scrimmage and three games of lightning, but they were still eager for more. At 7:00 p.m. on Friday after a full week of work, I pleaded, "Please boys, let's go home."

After practices, the team was my captive audience for "coach talk." I emphasized the importance of being at every practice and making a commitment to the team. This would require sacrifices from everyone: "Playing time will be reflected by your commitment, how hard you work, your improvement, and, last of all, your ability."

One of our first scrimmages was with Fatih College and it went well. We competed hard and played well as a team. I was impressed with our quickness and our ability to move up and down the court. I started those players who had been most faithful with their attendance—a stated emphasis of mine—and that meant that our best player, Efe, did not start. Everyone played, but to be candid, I could have played Efe less and Yiğit more, as he never missed practice. Yet, I made my point as Efe didn't start and he knew why. His absences were conflicts with the Club team that he also played on.

The highs and lows in my life as a coach made for frequent assessment of my career choice. Here my thoughts go back to that first-year scheduled scrimmage that was inexplicably cancelled. It was hard to hide my discouragement as I trudged down Mithatpaşa Avenue with a mesh bag full of basketballs slung over my shoulder. I was the hard-working Turk on his way home from work; the basketballs I carried replaced the typical worker's lunch pail and tools, but the strains of a day's work showed in my tired gait and sagging shoulders. My posture, however, was maybe more an indication of my frustration in the cancelled scrimmage than my fatigue. I had been a party to the "Turkish way" of doing things once again. If the kids were both-ered, they hid it well.

I recall one particular basketball practice shortened due to rain. After a short thirty-minute offensive drill, I quickly lined up everyone in an effort to make three successive free throws as a team. Not a difficult goal. Thirty-five minutes later, in total darkness and soaked from the rain, the boys finally came through with the consecutive free throws. The rain splashed our faces as we walked, laughing and talking, up the steps to our changing room. I felt closer to the team and they displayed more together-ness than at any other time that year.

A scrimmage match with 60 Yil Anadolu Lise—sixty *yil*, same age I was—was a good lesson for us. We found weaknesses in our transition defense, blocking out strategy, floor balance, and ball movement. Nevertheless, the players continued to be a pleasure to coach. They had a good attitude, respected each other, played hard, and learned rapidly. Basically, we were 10th graders playing 11th and 12th graders.

My players loved the game, and that made coaching enjoyable. There were no parents to deal with, no Title IX concerns, not even games to worry about. There were only kids who wanted to learn, play, and have fun. This was truly a unique coaching experience for an American coach. I am not saying that this system was the best or right one, but to my surprise the benefits of the Turkish system were becoming clearer to me. There is value in kids playing for their own interest and enjoyment. There were no college scholarships being waved around, no publicity to swell their heads, and no coaching egos to be stroked by compiling a winning record. It reminded me of how things were when I was a kid; I played for the sheer love of the game. My team in Turkey was playing for the simple pleasure of learning to be a player and to improve skills. I was also coaching for the right reasons—I wasn't certain if I was even getting paid.

By April, we had an opponent for our first Ministry game. My plan was to scout this opponent at a game in Karşiyaka—an area across the bay of Izmir. If I had a car, this outing would have been a thirty-minute drive. Since I didn't, I left the apartment at 8:00 a.m. for a 10:30 game.

This was my route as I left home—I walked down the street about four blocks to the bus stop, boarded a bus for a ten-minute ride to the ferryboat dock, hopped on a ferryboat for a thirty-five-minute trip across Izmir Bay, hailed a taxi, and, in my self-imposed broken Turkish accent, named the Karşiyaka Spor Salon as my destination. I arrived at a school and learned it was the wrong place. I hailed another taxi, went off to another location, and met no success. The cab driver took me to the taxi headquarters. After much discussion and phone calling, I was dropped off at the correct gym at 10:30 a.m., just in time to see the tip off. Our two opponents played a ragged and sloppy game. I concluded that both teams were beatable. We would have to play well though, for we were not good enough to win without being on our game.

The scouting experience was quite different from what I

was used to, even discounting the odd trip I took to find the gym. The same event in an American gym would have the following similarities—competition between two teams, spectators cheering loudly, if not sporadically, bad refereeing, coaches gesturing as they walked the sidelines, and the spirited play of the young. The differences? An old gym with a stage to the side, uniforms styled from years past, no band or cheerleaders, no student body or spectators except an occasional parent, and everyone looking the same (unlike the diversity one sees in America).

I did know this—I was ready for a game after approximately eighty practices. The team had improved and was ready as well, but only true competition would tell how much.

During our last practice before the big match on Saturday, we worked on the offensive and defensive sets and finished with shooting and conditioning. While the players were smart and caught on quickly, their instincts and grasp of the big picture were still lacking.

Game day and we played, we lost, we suffered! We did not deserve to win as we played selfishly and made poor decisions. We lost by two points on a three-point shot—it was more like a throw—that was taken at the buzzer from the mid court area. Fluke or not, we got what we deserved. I must share the blame. It was just a game, but I would see to it that we corrected these problems.

Our next practice went well. The team realized that they must concentrate on the fundamentals and on team play to be successful. Losing tends to get the attention of athletes and coaches in any country.

The tournament format was interesting . . . you know, "Only in Turkey." Teams from all over Izmir, hundreds of them, are placed in brackets of three. Each team plays the other two teams (called a round robin in America) and the team with the best record prevailed. But what if the teams each win one game—A beats B, C beats A, and B beats C? Well, just read on.

The pressure was on ACI. Our opponent had defeated the team that had beaten us by five points. We had lost by one point in our only game, so in order to advance, we had to win and win by a margin of six points.

We rode the bus, we played the game, and we won by nine points, 56–47. We played hard, we rebounded well, and our defense was awesome for a solid team effort.

Our victory meant that we were the team advancing in the playoff system. This produced another scouting adventure, allowing me to see regions of Izmir that I'd not explored. To scout our next opponents—Özel Turk College vs. Nacil Lise—I went to Buca, a forty-minute bus ride with only one transfer and no taxis or ferry trips necessary. The game was no contest. Nacil only had one very good player and he hampered the team by trying to do everything by himself.

Özel Turk, on the other hand, was an excellent team that had as much ability as any high school team I had ever seen. At this school, academics were not of paramount concern for the players; athletes were recruited to Özel Turk for the sole purpose of playing basketball. The players studied some but did not partake in the academic curriculum that the other students did. PE classes, for example, were relegated to outside courts and secondary gyms, so as not to disturb the play or practice of the basketball players. We had no chance against Özel Turk, but we could beat Nacil Lise with a good effort.

The day we played Özel Turk College my center didn't show up; on the same day, he'd been invited to try out for the Junior National Team. He had not told me he would miss our game, however. At half time, our best player came to ask if he could leave to go to the same try out. At least he asked. Two or three players from the other team also left, so that was that. I antici- pated such a thing happening, but when it did, I was shocked and disappointed. Students had a different approach to commit- ment and to the school team, but the precedent had obviously been set.

We were already beaten at half time, but I still felt badly. This cut-and-run action had diminished the other players, which I expressed to the team after the game. It was a disturbing way to end a season. We still had a game with Nacil Lise, so that competition would allow us to finish on a higher note. The two errant players assuredly would not start or play much. This was their country, with their rules, but I was the coach and would explain my philosophy on this issue one more time. I blamed the system more than I blamed the players. I couldn't change the system, but I could conceivably influence and interject some thought into the problems inherent with placing kids in such predicaments.

We played our final tournament game against Nacil Lise and won by a score of 45–37. We played man-to-man and doubled their 6'7" star player whenever he received a screen; he didn't like to pass, so that bothered him. We shot well from the outside, moved the ball well, and played as a team. I was happy for the kids. They had a long season with few games and many practices, and their effort was rewarded with a win.

When one of the players asked if I was returning next year, I said, "No, it doesn't look like it."

Ali, a young starter, said, "We will miss you. I really mean that!" With typical Turkish candidness, he added, "The team has been like a family to me." Ali was a good kid, a fine athlete, and a fierce competitor who would've been able to play on any team I had back home. I would miss the team too; their closeness to each other included me as the season progressed.

I believed I did the best I could for the team. We had practiced regularly from September through March. After tournaments concluded, we resumed practice in May as both coach and players were motivated to do so. We set goals that defined areas of improvement for each player. The final practice was an individualized workout, and I included a handout with fundamentals and drills for each player's workout schedule over the summer. The team had the potential to be good the following year. If I had been younger, I would have stayed just to coach them. They were the sort of kids I trusted to say and do the right thing, always a joy to be around. Their self-confidence was infectious and refreshing because it was not tinged with any arrogance, just a firm belief in self. In America, their attitude and presence might have a bit of a "swagger."

This group would most likely be the last team I would ever coach—a good way to end a coaching career.

ONLY IN TURKEY

The most unusual day we spent in Turkey was undoubtedly Census Day. The announcement—tacked to the school post office bulletin board—stated:

> **Census Day will be Sunday the 12th**
> **No one can leave their home between**
> **5:00 a.m. – 7:00 p.m.**

My first reaction was disbelief. Then came questions from the rest of the foreign faculty:

- "What are they saying? No one can leave their home?"
- "How can they make you stay home?"
- "Who will enforce this?"

The questions, while elementary in content, were inconsequential to the Turks. This was a culture that respected authority and did what it was told to do. Rights be damned, no exceptions, on Sunday the 12th, everyone would be at home. The entire country would stay home and wait for the census takers to visit. Even today I find Census Day hard to believe.

You would think that I could have relaxed and enjoyed a day off, yet the day was not calming, and I certainly could not relax.

The silence somehow seemed wrong. I was bothered to the point that I became nervous and walked to the window several times to see no one outside. After a long and boring morning, we heard a knock on the door. At last, we were to be counted. Three people, one who spoke English, entered. They appeared to know who we were and asked us several questions about our background and our time spent in Turkey. While we were discussing the written form, we heard talking outside. One census taker rushed to the window to see three men in an otherwise empty street. He yelled at them in Turkish, of course. I assumed he told them to get home, for they quickly disappeared around the corner.

The day was unlike any I had ever experienced. The ordinarily busy streets were empty and silent—no vendors sold their wares and no cars ceaselessly honked their way through the narrow streets. Even the dogs were quiet, and the cats were undisturbed in the garbage cans.

The following day the newspaper featured a front-page picture of a stark and empty midday street in downtown Istanbul. Can this oddity be found only in Turkey?

Sports Building

A final meeting with the architect and building consultant for the new sports arena left me relieved, but also puzzled. As usual, the Turkish mentality surprised me. The decision was reached to build a building that would not quite meet official specifications in regards to floor size and ceiling height. The rationale for the decision was not to save money or cut corners, but to keep the Turkish Ministry at bay. Therefore, a big, beautiful sports building would have a ceiling too low to house competitive volleyball tournaments and a floor too short for basketball competition. I don't know if I respected the decision, but I did understand it. (When things like this start to make sense, it might be time to go home.)

Here's the rationale behind the decision—when the

Ministry chose a gym as a tournament site, they commandeered the facility. As a result, the school must sacrifice their school programs and their students' participation for the glory of the Turkish Ministry and their tournaments. In their wisdom, ACI built an arena that would not meet tournament specifications and, as a result, would not have that problem. What could I say?

Long Hours

Jean and I walked by the sea in our neighborhood and stopped at our favorite pastry shop, Şortan. One particular Turkish worker loved to speak English and was always our personal waiter. When we came, even if he was waiting on someone else, he always gave us a smile and ignored his other customers to take care of us. At times he even sat with us and philosophized until his manager gave him the sign to get back to work. We loved the shop because it was clean, had good food, and employed our new friend.

We were saddened to learn that he was leaving to work at the Hilton. He worked seven days a week, about seventy hours, all with no overtime pay. He had no time to be with his family. This was the life for many Turks. The days in retail were often long and boring, as well. Would working at the Hilton be any different? I didn't think so.

American Sports Come To Turkey

One night, I slept for about half an hour and then got up to watch the Final Four. The school had bought a TV for our lounge and, as luck would have it, cable had just been installed. I watched the Final Four games from 12:30 a.m. until 6:00 a.m., my second set of games in a year. Somehow, I thought I was a better person for having watched them. I can still delude myself when necessary.

This experience was a far cry from the previous year when

another teacher and I wanted to watch the Super Bowl. We had gotten up at 1:00 a.m., brought snacks, bundled up at the hall where the TV was located—the room was not heated—and prepared to watch the game. We sat there in blankets eating chips and dip, pretzels, and drinking coke, but no game. Being either slow learners or overly optimistic (how about desperate), we waited for nearly two hours before giving up and returning to our homes. Still, it had felt like old times at the Met Stadium in Minneapolis as I trudged home with cold feet and a full stomach.

On the Bus

I had a Turkish experience on the bus one day that I would never understand. A passenger in the back, upset with the driver, began a loud conversation with him, yelling to be heard over all the other passengers. The bus made a stop, and the passenger stepped out the back exit door. Once outside, he walked to the front door, got back on the bus, and resumed the argument, now face to face with the driver. As the bus continued on its route, a female passenger joined in the heated exchange of words. Five minutes later, another eight to ten people joined the debate. The verbal brouhaha attracted the attention of those on the street, who looked up in wonder at the commotion coming from the moving bus. People were up in their seats, gesturing excitedly, shouting loudly. The driver reciprocated; occasionally, he watched the road. Finally, most of the people either left the bus or moved to the back. Suddenly it was quiet. No wailing. No talking. Silence. I sat in wonder at what I had witnessed. It was another one of those times I yearned for the ability to better understand the language.

At the Dentist

At my first experience with a Turkish dentist, I shook hands with a ruggedly handsome man with large physical features and a soft manner. I concluded that extensive x-rays, heavy drilling, and possibly a tooth extraction would follow his examination. However, his thorough but brief examination determined that my sore gum line and throbbing tooth were caused by food infection, a diagnosis that proved to be accurate.

Prior to this day, I had received good news from the dentist only twice in my life, both while I was fairly young. The first good news was from Dr. Pete who called my home to cancel my appointment for several fillings (of course to be done without Novocain). My parents thought his reason was suspect, but I was thrilled. The second set of good news occurred when a dentist determined that I had only two wisdom teeth—not four—and, hence, only needed to pull the two. Now, in Turkey of all places, I received my third piece of favorable news from a dentist. His diagnosis and advice to improve my flossing would rank up there with the other two unforgettable dental moments.

As I was about to leave the dentist chair, he motioned to a chair beside his desk. He wanted to talk. Now that I knew he wouldn't hurt me, I would have complied with anything. The lack of throbbing in my tooth was also a good sign. As we sipped tea and he smoked a cigarette, we visited about children, educational goals, and life in general. He shared that he would likely be sending his two children to the United States for their university training.

The contrast with an American dental office was evident from the moment I walked in the door. I appreciate our assembly-line approach for its efficiency and effectiveness. I enjoyed the Turkish way for its intimacy and personal touch. If I had been offered a cigar, I would have really been impressed and possibly become a convert to Turkish dentistry.

At the Races

One afternoon, Jean and I were among a few Turks and foreigners who went to the track for a horseracing debut. The weather was cool, the picker was hot.

In a nine-horse race midway through the schedule, I picked horses number three and six to win and place. Jean picked number six to place as well. The bets were entered by our Turkish friend, and we were off to watch the race. We cheered our picks to a Win and a Place! We could retire! We ran to the lady who placed our bets, and found everyone huddled around her at our chosen meeting place.

They all turned as I announced with obvious enthusiasm, "We won, we won!"

Unforgivably, a member of the group gazed at me with more of a sneer than a smile and said, "No you didn't. She couldn't place all the bets on time. Here is your money back."

I didn't want my money back; I wanted my winnings. If the truth were known, I also wanted the bragging rights that went along with my earnings!

Betting had lost its appeal. We decided to move on to the next part of our schedule—tea and conversation at the adjacent saddle club. A less participatory role was fine with me after the emotional distress. Only in Turkey!

Beautification Comes to the Neighborhood

Sitting on my balcony early one beautiful morning, my attention was drawn to a man across the way. He was busy pulling up flowers from various beds that were already quite sparse. I watched with interest as he went from flowerbed to flowerbed. Suddenly he was gone, so I returned to my reading and thought little of what had taken place . . . until later in the day when I returned from grocery shopping. What a surprise to see our horticulturist neighbor in action again, this time in a barren plot two blocks from our apartment. Now, presumably in his own garden, he was favoring it with what appeared to be a new selection of plants, but were quite familiar-looking flowers. One by one, he placed them in the ground. I call it beautifying the neighborhood, one stolen flower at a time. After watching for a few minutes, I called out, "*Çok güzel*" (very beautiful) and walked away. My only thought was that if he didn't care for them properly, I would turn flower-informer.

A Last Trip to Çeşme

Belma's cottage in Çeşme was about four blocks from the sea, and I was up early to pursue one of my favorite activities—a walk by the water. I enjoyed anonymity while walking in strange and unknown territory. Few were out this early in the morning, which resulted in less distraction and more peace. This would be our last trip to Çeşme, and my mind was filled with nostalgia as I walked.

As the morning shifted into afternoon, it was siesta time in Çeşme. I decided I would take advantage of the moment by kicking back and reading on a low-lying chair on Belma's patio. In my relaxed state, I quickly fell into a deep, sound sleep. Abruptly, a loud "crack" zapped me awake, as my chair went crashing to the ground. As I fell backward, my arms flew up, bumping the wooden clothes rack, which, in turn, fell down on my head, opening a small cut on my forehead. Several people, as astonished as I, came running to investigate the noise. Blood streamed down my face as I struggled to rise from my awkward position on the ground—not an easy movement even if had I been operating with my full senses. Belma's daughter, Başak, urged me to the kitchen to do something to stop the bleeding.

A command then came from Belma. "Come, follow me."

Pulled upright, I stood frozen. "I can't move," I said weakly.

"What's wrong?" Belma asked, her attention at high alert (along with everyone else's).

"I can't move my leg."

Belma was probably thinking that I was a typical, quick-to-sue American who would now go home rich and disabled. Well, neither was the case, as the awkward and somewhat contorted position in my miniature lounge chair had caused my legs to go numb, or as we used to say in my hometown of Benson (and everywhere else), "My leg went to sleep."

Everyone was now hysterical with laughter, and I had no other option but to join in with them. A little movement, a little ice, and I was on the road to recovery. I usually like making people laugh, but this was taking it to extremes.

It's Show Time

Attending a movie in Turkey allowed us to see currently released American films at a reasonable price. The whole movie package included a reserved seat, a strobe light show that was decidedly Turkish in its flamboyance, English-speaking movies with Turkish subtitles, and the smallest bag of popcorn in the world. We didn't go often, but it always made for an entertaining night out.

On one particular movie evening, we had an especially interesting experience. Earlier, during a shopping outing, Jean had purchased some black-olive-and-grapevine-patterned dishes— cups, saucers, bowls, the works. This purchase filled four large shopping bags, which we carried with us into the theater.

We found that our reserved seats were in the middle of a crowded row without room to stock-pile our bags of dishes. Well, our culture took over and we did the American thing—we moved. We found two seats up high, in the corner, where there was room to stash our packages. We were feeling quite comfortable in our "select suite" as the theater darkened and the light show began.

Our comfort level changed when we saw the usher moving toward us with his flashlight followed by two people looking for their seats, which were, of course, just where we were sitting. The flashlight was now on us and, as I tried to explain, it became clear to them that I did not speak Turkish. I gestured to the mound of packages scattered around, and they obliged us by backing away to search for the seats that had been assigned to us—front row middle. I loved this country.

Uninhibited Student Action

As a teacher, meeting your students in the American public can bring a variety of reactions. They may ignore you and look the other way, or they might be embarrassed and offer a shy greeting. On occasion in America, I had experienced both the formal greeting, "Hi Mr. Johnson," and the look that said, "Why are you out in public anyway?"

While Christmas shopping in modern and trendy Alsancak, we met several students as they were leaving their weekend cram school. These were Lise (senior) students who did not let age inhibit their behaviors. Upon seeing Jean they chanted, "Mrs. Johnson, computer teacher," clap, clap, clap. Then it was my turn: "Mr. Johnson, best coach," clap, clap, clap. Pedestrians took notice. The students acted without the least bit of self-consciousness.

Note: this behavior was displayed not only to us but also to all teachers as a show of affection for teachers in general.

Tradition Is Everything

Circumcision is a religious tradition that all Turkish boys undergo between the ages of five and fifteen. The operation is considered a turning point from childhood to manhood. Most parents don't wish to break away from this entrenched custom. Recently, however, in the bigger cities, some parents have children circumcised in the hospital immediately after birth.

We were never invited to a circumcision celebration, but observed many from afar. I understood that the operation could take place at home or in a rented facility when more than one was being performed. For days in advance, and perhaps also for mental preparedness, the boys were seen wearing white trousers and white shirts. On the day of the affair, they donned a white cape and a white sailing-type cap.

Several circumcision parties took place on the streets of our neighborhood. These events were all accompanied by a band, dancing, food, gifts, and the finale, the "ride." The "ride" would be the highlight as the boy(s) would parade around town in an old 1958 red Chevrolet convertible rented for the occasion. Every circumcision party we observed used the same car—or one of a comparable year and color—to lead the celebration. The boys were conspicuous in their white uniform, perched high on the back of the convertible as they traveled the town, waving and basking like royalty. Cars would join the procession to honor this religious ritual.

The circumcision ceremony is enhanced with gifts of money, clothing, and material items. In traditional communities, serious attention is paid to inviting everybody.

Death

Death produces grief in any culture, and we learned tragically the traditions and rituals connected with the Islamic faith our first year. An Orta 1 student was killed in a bus accident on her way to school. A student in Jean's computer class, she was a wonderful girl with a bright future. Her death and burial the same day brought to our attention the similarities and differences in our religions and cultures.

Islam, as with most faiths, view death as a natural part of life. Interment in a cemetery is a shared custom, but in Islam the person who died must be buried as soon as possible and during the daylight. If the death occurs at night, burial has to take place early the next day. Friends are encouraged to visit the house of the deceased, share memories, and talk about the circumstances of the death. Coffins are used and the body is wrapped in a clean white shroud after cleansing. The funeral, conducted in the Mosque and led by the Imam, is for grieving and for remembering the deceased with kind words and expressions of faith and prayer.

Traditions differ in every country, and the Turkish interpretation of Islam is in some ways different from those in other Muslim countries.

CRUNCH TIME
AND SCHOOL DAYS

Spring had arrived. It was time to teach my Prep students some softball. The only problem was that they knew literally nothing about softball—they had never even watched a baseball game. Watching them play on this particular day—after teaching only three class periods of skills and concepts—was like scanning a video on rewind. What could I expect?

When a batter hit the ball, fair or foul, players ran randomly to any base. As kids flew around the bases, the excitement picked up, and the ball was thrown wildly from player to player. The noise level grew with each second, and the runners and throwers in their excitement forgot—if they ever knew—about tagging runners, throwing to bases, and forcing outs. One student, with the ball in hand, looked up in panic to see a runner coming right at her. I instinctively yelled, "Tag her!" Well, she went with her instincts, which told her to throw the ball directly at the runner. Her lack of throwing skill, plus the fact that she was screaming wildly and jumping skittishly, was opportune, and the ball struck the runner softly on the thigh. We had worked on the fundamentals of throwing, catching, and hitting, but I was wrong with my conclusion that they would actually learn the game by playing. Because of their hyper-by-nature personality, the game quickly became bedlam. The perspiration of the young Turks left vapor trails as they flew about. I was the traffic cop caught in a situation where only gridlock would slow down the confusion. It would get better. It had to.

Where's Your Tie?

Near the end of our second year, when summer vacation was on the horizon, the staff began to crack down on uniforms. Summer uniforms meant the boys were not required to wear jackets and the girls were not required to wear sweaters. Slippage occurred in the form of boys not wearing ties and leaving shirts untucked. The girls learned to shorten their skirts by rolling them at the waist, and they also left their blouses untucked.

Because of the careless dress, all students were notified that the following Monday would be a full uniform day. The instructions stated that any student not wearing the proper uniform would be sent home. How would this be enforced? I read somewhere that Turks didn't like to follow rules but did adhere to customs. We had three gates of entry to the school. They were manned by security guards day and night. Well, on Monday, students passing through each of the gates would do so at the approval of two school deans. Any uniform violation would result in the student being sent home to change.

Sound extreme? Apparently, a few years back, the school made the decision during a warm spell to allow students to dress in shorts and causal shirts. As a result, the students' behavior caused so many problems that the summer dress policy was rescinded and full-uniform wear was immediately reinstated. Is this anecdote cause to mandate uniforms in the United States? Would uniforms result in better behavior and more learning? My answer? Yes, it's worth a try.

The stage was set. As the students arrived on Monday morning, they found six deans (including me) posted at three separate gates of entry to the ACI campus. Students were surprised to see their deans and cheerfully called out as they approached. After paying his taxi cab fare, my star basketball player walked toward me wearing a friendly smile, gray slacks, white shirt, and Navy blazer.

"Osman, where is your tie?" I asked.

"It's in my locker," he replied.

I hesitated. The Lise dean spoke up, "Too bad. You'll have to go home and get another one."

Osman was shocked and speechless; I was just speechless. She continued, "You know the rules, you should have put your tie on and had it with you when you left home."

Apparently, students had ties stashed around. And come to think of it, we had a few abandoned ties in our office. He looked at me for help, but to no avail; I was not in control of the situation at this point. He turned and hailed the taxi from which a group of five students had just departed. Without a word or glance backward, he was off on a forty-minute ride to retrieve his tie.

The process continued as student after student was asked to go home and get the white shirt, correct blouse, tie, or whatever item was missing. My particular gate sent home nine students that morning. It was noteworthy to observe how the students accepted our actions. It was equally remarkable when I saw Osman later in the school day with the missing tie now properly in place. He didn't say a word about it, while I felt uncomfortable. Others also appeared to accept the action and harbored no grudge. The Turkish people were not wimpy, but they were not contentious either.

The seniors had their first graduation marching practice and, as usual, some were late! Cultural differences sprang up every day and in many ways. As the marching order was being established, I was again disappointed to find that the order was determined by height. The tallest boys and girls were at the beginning of the line, graduating down to the smallest at the end. It was a surprise that the boys were the shortest and made up the last five spots in the marching order. They were in full panic mode as they stretched and stood on their tiptoes to escape that last spot. I am not politically correct by most standards, but this was not right. What was wrong with marching in alphabetical order? Or, why not march based on class rank? My cultural response was . . . what a thoughtless system! Their response to my criticism and suggestion for change was that this was tradition.

The first round of the University Exams results were in—all our students passed except one. The second round was in June, and the number of students would be paired down to the number of openings in the various universities.

The last day for the seniors meant reduced stress levels for all concerned. The seniors weren't bad, but the general feeling was, to quote a teacher, "The sooner they are gone, the fewer problems there will be, and the better the school will run." This could be said of every senior class, in every school, in every year, and in every country.

To celebrate the end of the school year, the younger students had put together a film festival of their own work. It was patterned after the Academy Awards Ceremony and afforded the students another opportunity to perform in English. They were marvelous with their poise, their flair for dramatics, and their ability to perform in their second language. Test weeks were to begin the following Monday, so this event was a good stress reliever.

If it seemed as though every day was an event, it was, because every day brought one. Bazaar Day was a fundraiser with a carnival atmosphere—food, entertainment, and games. If you wanted to ride on a camel, eat cotton candy, or hear a live rock band, Bazaar Day had it all. The feature attraction was the Turkish rock band Athena. They were quite good, one of the hottest in Turkey, and they played to a full and raucous house in the amphitheater. There was even a Turkish version of a mosh pit. The performance energized the entire crowd and a thousand or more students clapped, danced, and sang along. This was my first rock concert since the Beach Boys in 1984 at the Minnesota State Fair. Every twenty years should do it. I now had two CDs to enjoy.

At the director's request, I called the two people back in the United States who would replace me the following year. We talked at length, and I was straightforward with them. It was not possible to do justice about such an emotional, life-changing experience in a phone conversation with someone I had never met. I even found myself becoming envious of them, which could be another reason to leave Turkey. (I had always wanted to return home when I was still enjoying the experience.) As I hung up the phone, I was overcome with good thoughts and a wistful feeling—part of me yearned to change my mind about leaving.

A Turkish Graduation

Jen graduated with her Turkish peers, the only foreigner in the class. The amphitheater set the scene for a beautiful ceremony as the sun lazily set over the relaxed yet impressive atmosphere. The graduation mood was upbeat and very respectful of tradition—family, school, and country. Jennifer appeared to enjoy and appreciate the moment. She stood amidst the 114 Turks, all of whom had forged fast friendships during their six years at ACI. Jen had a few close friends and many acquaintances. She must have had some doubts about being in Turkey and graduating from ACI, but hopefully, the positives outweighed the negatives, particularly in the long term. We were so proud of her spirit and the fact she survived the struggle through her discipline and work ethic. It was also special for Jen to have Kurt present at her graduation to cheer her on and make it a family event. After tea and pastries on the grounds, we were home by 11:30 p.m. Jen opened a few presents, the four of us talked and drank more tea, and the high school graduation celebration in Turkey was complete. In the fall, she would begin college at the University of Virginia.

Finish Strong

I had my last day with my seventh grade guidance class. They were a very interesting, energetic, and sometimes crazy bunch of twelve boys and twelve girls. From big, outspoken, husky Yiğit to the quiet, studious, brilliant Yilmaz, they were each so different. In their six years until graduation, they would experience so much together. They would defend and protect each other, as family members do. They would express pride in each other's achievements, tolerate weaknesses, and show love openly and without embarrassment.

The Blake House was the scene of a lovely lunch on the flower-laden patio. I invited the physical education staff to a well-presented chicken stir-fry, with tossed salad, hard bread, and Turkish wine. We had all been through some trying times in these two years and this was a way to reflect in a relaxed and informal setting. All of us had grown comfortable in our struggle to communicate with each other. We sat and reminisced, laughed, and shared an emotion or two. It was also an opportunity for me to express my thanks for their support. If I were to start my own school, I would hire this group without hesitation. It would have been easier if we had spoken the same language, but I wouldn't have changed the experience of working with them.

I continued to finish my responsibilities—grading, cleaning up, and bringing the year to a close. Everyone else was off and running; I was savoring the last moments of two meaningful years.

I spent much of the next day in a meeting with the Lise dean. We assessed the year, and I offered my insight for future improvements. She was a willing learner who wanted to be successful in her new job. She had been in education only a few years as a result of a late-age job change. I admired her courage and willingness to take risks and make decisions that, while unpopular, needed to be made. She presented herself well and was an extremely hard worker. It was my thought that as she gained experience, she would develop a sense for viewing the big picture and would learn how to delegate her authority. She would probably run the school some day.

On the last day of school, in the library attempting to complete my grading and ordering for next year, I was surprised by the sudden arrival of several students from one of my Prep classes. They began pasting stickers on me that said "the tallest teacher," "the tallest and friendliest teacher," "the funniest teacher," and finally, "the most helpful teacher." This must have been their last project before school let out. They really enjoyed themselves and so did I. Report cards were handed out, pictures taken, and hugs distributed. School was out!

One advantage of teaching in a private school is the appreciation shown by the Turks, which they display often and with great fanfare. Several hundred people had joined us to say goodbye. A farewell party atop the library terrace was the setting for a dinner and dance on a starlit evening. Each departing teacher was given a gift, along with an individual expression of thanks and acknowledgement. The lively music from the band provided the grand finale for the evening as we danced both American and Turkish style.

The last party we celebrated was the "Ball of 98" at the Efes Hotel. This was an exclusive party in an elegant courtyard to honor the Class of 1998. A special memory for me was the first dance of the night between the student and his or her parent—girls danced with their fathers, and boys with their mothers. So Jen and I danced, a proud moment for me. Jennifer had assessed many of life's questions and personal inventories throughout her two years in Turkey. She would be stronger as a person with improved skills to cope with what life offered her. I envied the lessons she learned at this early age.

OVERTIME

Religion and Law

The population in Turkey is 99 percent Muslim, mostly of the Sunni creed. The remaining one percent consists of Greek Orthodox, Jews, Catholics, and Protestants. The Muslim physical presence is ubiquitous with mosques and spiral, sky-reaching minarets looming prominently above every village and city. The Call to Prayer emanates from the mosques five times a day. The basic Muslim beliefs are that God (Allah) created the world just as the Bible states and that the Koran is their sacred book. Muslims accept Adam, Noah, Abraham, Moses, and Jesus as important prophets. They take exception, however, with Christianity's belief in Jesus as divine Savior. Muslims believe Muhammad was the greatest and last prophet. He is not believed to be divine, but he is God's messenger; so they believe and worship God, not Muhammad.

The five duties of a Muslim are to:

1. Believe that there is no god but Allah

2. Pray five times daily

3. Give aid to the poor

4. Keep the fast at Ramadan during daylight hours, if possible

5. Make one pilgrimage to Mecca, if possible

Most of our Turkish neighbors adhered to some of these practices, but not all. For instance, they may not have prayed five times a day, but during Ramadan they gave aid to the poor. This aid was most often rendered by the purchase and sharing of a lamb. During Ramadan, we saw small groups of lambs being herded about and offered for sale in random locations around the city. We would later also notice these animals hanging on balconies after they had been slaughtered. That was a shocking and unpleasant sight for us, along with the streams of blood flowing through the streets; but it was tradition and done with benevolence. The Turks that we interacted with every day, however, were more secular and so they did not follow many of these traditions.

I read the book *The Loom of History*, about the life of Kemal Mustafa Atatürk, the father of modern-day Turkey. He had the foresight that allowed him to lay the groundwork for this country. He also possessed the courage to create a democracy precluding the Muslim religion from ruling the government. This proved to be critical for Turkey's development and growth into a modern and developed country—at least for the most part. Today, Islamic law is *the* law in most Muslim countries. Turkey, however, is the exception; secular law replaced Islamic law in 1923 under Atatürk. Since that time, the army has enforced secular law by constitutional mandate.

Can Christians Find Happiness in a Muslim Country?

We have discussed the emotional and psychological impact of foreign living. I was not, however, prepared for the spiritual changes that came my way. These changes and influences were not a conflict between Islam and Christianity, but an example of being in need of the strength and support that one's belief system can provide.

We worshiped freely in an Anglican church, which was associated with the Church of England. Each Sunday, two armed guards were stationed at the front gate of the church. The reason for their presence remained a mystery to us and, although it was initially unsettling, we never felt in danger or uncomfortable as we worshipped.

The U.S. military was also allowed to hold church services off base. In one instance, they used a facility that was rented from the Turkish government. It was my understanding that the more fundamental elements in the eastern part of Turkey would not be as tolerant. There have been several documented incidents of persecution and death against Christians in Turkey in the past ten years, but the instances appear to be isolated and not a reflection of any governmental position.

My writing about Christianity is not intended to be a journal of my walk of faith. Yet the unusual amount of time we had to reflect and read bombarded me with information, thoughts, doubts, fears, and circumstances that, at home in the United States, I didn't take the time to consider. In Turkey, I found myself thinking more about life's meaning and the purpose for my life. Here, I seemed to listen better and the stories of the ancient world clearly spoke to me. From biblical and historical figures like Noah, Paul, and Homer, to the cities of Ephesus and Troy, we were physically inundated with the history of the past six thousand years. When I walked in St. Paul's footsteps and realized that I knew little of his life or impact on the world, I wanted to know more. In II Corinthians 12:10, Paul wrote, "I delight in weaknesses because when I am weak, then I am strong." I learned from Paul, a native of Tarsus, Turkey, that we all struggle to find our way. Life is always difficult, but more so when you live in a different culture. My understanding is that when we struggle or suffer we are changed, and this leads to a strengthened faith. Did our minimal struggles in Turkey bring us closer to God?

Personally, I felt more accountable to my Christian faith while in Turkey and more answerable for staying connected to God. Any growth or maintenance in my faith was my responsibility. God was here, but my church, my pastors, and my Christian friends and support groups were not.

What did I do to take more responsibility for my faith? My knowledge of the Bible was not strong nor had I been successful at studying it over my many years. I had been in several Bible studies, but I never felt that my faith was strengthened; I had only learned the nominal Christian beliefs that I thought would make me a better husband and father. In Turkey, however, I had to take the initiative to learn more, as the Anglican Church in Alsancak was not a strong Bible-teaching church. Someone had given me the One-Year Bible, which was organized to read selected portions of the Old and New Testaments each day, along with a verse from Proverbs. This reading was part of my quiet time each morning. I felt better prepared to walk out the door and face my new surroundings when I had that time to read, think, and pray.

The Old Testament was a hard place for me to find relevance, and quite honestly, I didn't always understand it. I needed someone to discuss with and share with me, but I didn't reach out in that way. Another struggle came from the fact that I wasn't making the proper connections between the Old and New Testament. The fact that much of the Old Testament is about Jesus was something I had never figured out. I was, however, in the proper place to make those connections. Turkey is called the "Cradle of Civilization;" it's where Noah's ark was reported to be found at Mt. Ararat and it's where St. Paul preached and began spreading Christianity two thousand years ago. Paul wrote much of the New Testament after Christ died, spending time at Ephesus—a short distance from the city of Izmir. The fact that he wrote, taught, and preached there provided me the relevance

I needed.

What then did I learn? I learned a Christian can practice his or her faith in a Muslim country.

TIMEOUT—BLACK SEA

For our last big trip within the country, we were advised that the Black Sea would offer us the best overall experience. With twenty Turks, several ACI students and their parents, and three friends, we were off on a ten-day bus trip. Izmir sat on the West Coast of the Aegean Sea; we would begin by traveling eastward to Ankara, the capital of Turkey, located in the heart of the Anatolian plateau. Ankara is a planned city with wide streets and boule-vards presenting a modern appearance, but its origins can be traced back to the 6th century B.C.

Bus travel in Turkey is world class—First World class. Most buses seem new and are impressive with their Mercedes Benz engines purring quietly in the midst of Turkey's blaring traffic. The inside features all the comforts of home. On any tourist bus in Turkey there is a male attendant who escorts people on and off, serves drinks, checks on tickets, and is a genuine help to the passengers. After the boarding tasks are completed and the bus is underway, the attendant walks the aisle with a bottle of *Limon Kolonyasi*, a Turkish product offered to everyone in liberal doses. On my first bus trip I watched with skepticism as he approached; not certain of what I was offered, I was cautious. Demonstrating with my thumb and forefinger, I said in my limited Turkish, "*Biraz, lütfen*" (a little please). The zesty lemon aroma was prom-inent, but not offensive. Soon the bus smelled like a French elevator, which would be unacceptable in a politically correct country like the United States. But after I had walked to catch a taxi in the warm sun, stood in line to purchase tickets and board, and lugged a few bags in the process, this cologne was the perfect anecdote. I found that the more I traveled by bus, the more *kolonyasi* I lavished on myself. I began as a dabbler; I became a splasher. Brushing my hands on my face and through my hair, I splashed the liquid down my neck to complete the journey. I still have a bottle of *Limon Kolonyasi* in my cabinet at home. Subconsciously I may be waiting for that next bus trip.

The bus window displayed for me an orderly countryside with rows of crops. A contrast was evident between farms, however. One had a modern combine carefully picking up the downed windrows. The adjacent field had a threshing machine as old as I was, with workmen picking up the fallen grain with their giant-sized pitchforks. The women-folk stacked the grain for the men to pick up and deliver to the threshing machine. The scene brought back memories from the 1950s on my grandpa's farm.

We were approaching the Black Sea when we left our comfortable bus and boarded four minvans for an hour-long trip to a mountain top. The imposing mountain featured trees, waterfalls, and ensuing streams. The minivans meandered up the winding road, while we viewed the grandeur of the mountain. We passed a few small logging ventures on our way, and the sound of chain saws and trucks moving about interrupted the otherwise tranquil scene. The few workers we saw were focused on their job and paid little attention to our small caravan. Eventually, the forest turned into a vast and grassy clearing of land where grazing sheep and goats greeted us. Unexpectedly the land was plateau-like, the temperature was comfortable, and only the inaccessibility for equipment would preclude farming the land.

But it was the sheepherder squatting down in the grass that captured our interest. He paid no attention to us and seemed lost in his thoughts. Or, he might have been bored with the tourists that came his way.

Small in stature, he appeared much older as we drew nearer.

He was dressed warmly with a woolen sweater under a pink hooded sweatshirt, his boots were made for harsh conditions, and the blue denim hat with a short visor in front and a longer flap in the back gave him protection from the sun. With an offer of money, he allowed us to take his picture. His ease in posing gave us the distinct feeling that this wasn't his first modeling stint. Since then and more than once I have thought of his lonely life and the means he had developed to cope. Maybe my feeling of sadness for him was unwarranted.

As we moved on, the countryside became awash in vegetation. Compared to the arid lands we had become accustomed to, this area was a pleasant change. The plentiful rainfall in the Black Sea region made the tea fields glimmer emerald-like on bright summer days. To quote a local devotee, an "imminent social collapse" would result from a tea shortage or crop failure.

In the fields, the workers, mostly women, used their skill and balance to work the machete-like knives to chop the leaves off the plants, all the while staying upright and navigating the steep mountain slopes. While in Turkey, learning to drink and appreciate tea changed my life. To quote the phrasing on my tea bag, "Indulging in the soothing ritual of tea brings a new dimension to life. No calories, carbs, or fat." (And don't forget about the antioxidants.)

Teaching English to a young Turkish soldier became a daily routine on our trip. He wanted to learn words that he could pronounce and use properly in sentences and conversation. He sat apart from me in the front of the bus practicing his new words. When the bus stopped and my foot hit the ground, he was there ready to recite. The next step was to place the words into sentence form—"The view is awesome," and, "The harbor is quiet." He was relentless and always upbeat. A quick learner and fine young man, he continued to correspond with us for two years, beginning each letter with, "Dear Mr. Craig."

Toward the end of the trip, while drinking a coke at a rest stop, my soldier friend leaned forward and softly asked with his ever-improving English, "Can I ask of you a question?"

"I was wondering of two questions," he said, his accent quite pronounced. "Why do American soldiers use [a particular swear word] all the time?" And, "Who do you think is worse, 'Beel' Clinton or Saddam Hussein?"

Looking me right in the eye, his sincerity told me he wanted an answer. I stammered out a reply: "The soldiers are away from home and are mostly around men. They tend to become careless and develop bad speech habits."

Quickly, I moved on to his second question and answered, "Bill Clinton had an affair, but unlike Hussein, he has not killed anyone."

He nodded in agreement. There was the notion in my mind that the questions were as much political as personal. Maybe he belonged to the Turkish Army Intelligence Division. Or, maybe I'm becoming overly suspicious.

The streets of Safranboğlu were alive on our early morning walk. The fresh air invited open doors and windows, and the morning sun brought comfortable warmth to the day. A woman swept her front entrance with the standard back-breaking short-handled broom. The broom required the user to bend severely at the waist while keeping their short legs straight. While straddling the broom, quick little rapid motions made the dust fly. I hoped these brooms were not recommended by the Chiropractic Society of Turkey. Any user taller than five feet would be at risk for back trouble.

Safranboğlu was noted for its Ottoman-style homes. Their peaked roofs, shuttered windows, and decorated balconies gave them a cottage look, which was a shift from the boxy, cement homes of Izmir. Down the street, four men sat on a bench drinking tea. After a wave and a verbal gesture of friendship, I was invited to join them. Picture three of the four men with mustaches, two wearing hats (one a fedora), and two with sports coats and checked pants. They were dressed for a funeral, a wedding, shopping, or sipping tea with friends—so very Turkish.

Me, I was in shorts and sandals, looking very unstylish—so American.

In my experience, riding a bus had always seemed to encourage singing, and the Turks often regaled us with traditional songs of Turkey. On one occasion, we were asked to sing American folk songs, and we all froze at the request. They asked again and our response was cold silence. Personally, I love sing-a-longs and campfire songs. It has puzzled me why I didn't step up to the plate, and that fact is a source of regret as I write this. "Home on the Range"—"You are My Sunshine"—"Someone's in the Kitchen with Dinah"—the list is endless. Is it too late for forgiveness?

POST-GAME ANALYSIS

During our two years in Turkey we fought a few battles; thankfully, we also stopped to eat some grapes. The impact of the choices we made at school—within Turkish culture—had a far-reaching effect. Hopefully, these choices benefited the lives of those we served.

To give an accurate assessment of our time in Turkey requires a heavy dose of subjectivity on my part. I must go beyond the stories and anecdotes to assess our experience of living and working in Turkey for two years. It requires me to look into my heart more than merely recalling events and happenings. On second thought, to eliminate excessive sentimentality, I will just express my admiration for the warmth and generosity that the Turkish people always showed us—fellow teachers, students, parents, and the community at large. My thanks goes to the Turks for accepting a group of foreigners into their workplace and homes with such openness.

The Prep students that I taught will have graduated from university by this time. They were academically prepared to excel, and they possess the leadership to apply their learning. They will make a difference in their country and in this world.

During current times, there is much to lament about. Yet there are young people everywhere just like those young Turks, ready to make this world a better and safer place; one filled with justice. They give us reason to be confident and hopeful.

A Final Walk

The parties were over and the bags had been packed. Now was the time to say good-bye to our home of two years. What better way to do that than a walk by the sea. The three of us walked slowly to our destination, a fresh fish restaurant situated on a man-made peninsula jutting into the Bay of Izmir. We were joined unexpectedly by a fellow teacher from Canada. A fresh sea bass dinner accompanied the reflections of two years as we ate and talked. We cherished the memories as much as our last meal in Turkey. On our final walk by the sea, my mood was pensive—a good word because it covers so many emotions. My feelings were all jumbled in the center, not on any extreme. In other words, there was no joy, no depression, but a discomfort that told me that things were going to be different, both for the good and the bad.

We crossed the road from the sea and walked by the countless buildings that faced the water. The smell of food—grilled lamb kebabs—was pungent in the nighttime air. The evening was at the height of activity—the balconies were alive with families eating their typically late-dinner meal. On the street the young were congregated to talk, drink, and smoke, as they casually sat by the small tables that most restaurants supplied. Vendors were busy selling everything from sweet corn to popcorn to jewelry. Jean and Jen each bought a last remembrance from Turkey—a pair of silver earrings. I felt safe in the numbers surrounding us, yet nowhere were there friends. People-watching was our entertainment; it was cheap, but good fun. We ultimately left behind the sounds and smells of the nighttime market and walked the three blocks to our apartment.

My thoughts of leaving Turkey turned inward. I didn't feel sadness as much as fear about leaving something behind that was so personal that I would never be able to adequately share it with others. Looking back, that proved to be true.

Until now.

ACKNOWLEDGEMENTS

Relationships are the essence of teaching and coaching, and each relationship contributed to the foundation of this book. Yet there are a few individuals I must particularly thank for the development and production of *Eat the Grapes*:

- To Jean and Jennifer for your willing spirits and sacrifice.

- To Jean for the photos that help visualize our story.

- To Craig and Heidi and Kurt and Bekah, for your encouragement, support, and willingness to join us on a leg of our two-year journey.

- To the students, teachers, and school workers from the American Collegiate Institute (ACI) who were the inspiration for the stories that comprise this book.

- To Beaver's Pond Press, and specifically Dara Beevas and Jay Monroe, for your mentoring and book design.

- To Cindy Rogers, my editor, for your thoughtful suggestions.

- To the happy memory of my parents, who, as teachers, modeled the profession well.

ALS

Amyotrophic lateral sclerosis (ALS), often referred to as Lou Gehrig's Disease, is a progressive, fatal neuromuscular disease that slowly robs a person of their ability to walk, speak, swallow, and breathe.

ALS can strike anyone at any time. The disease knows no racial, ethnic, or socioeconomic boundaries. The life expectancy of a person with ALS averages two to five years from the time of diagnosis.

In 1955 at the age of 46, Craig L. Johnson (my father) died of ALS. In 1985 at the age of 77, Ingvald Moe (Jean's father), also died of ALS.

A portion of the sale of each book will be donated to the ALS Association to improve patient services and advance research.

For more information, contact www.alsmn.org,
or call 888.672.0484.

ABOUT THE AUTHOR

Craig Johnson is a first-time author and lifelong educator. His thirty-nine-year career ended in Izmir, Turkey, which is the subject of this book. He is retired and he and his wife Jean live in Minneapolis.

Since returning from Turkey, Jean has been working for the Hennepin County Library System as a technology trainer.

Jennifer graduated from the University of Virginia. She spent two years teaching English in Japan and then received a Master's degree in theological studies from Bethel Seminary. She presently works in communications for a church in Minneapolis.